SPANISH CHATBOOK 1

chat•book (*chat-bůk*) —*noun* **1** : Our first-level conversational workbook with Spanish lessons

BY

JULIE JAHDE POSPISHIL

AND

BRADLEY POSPISHIL

SpanishChatCompany.com
Omaha, Nebraska

Revised edition February 2018

Copyright © 2017 by Spanish Chat Company

The original Spanish Chatbook was first published in 2011

All rights reserved. No part of this book may be reproduced or transmitted in any form or by any means, electronic or mechanical, including photocopying, recording, or by any information storage and retrieval system, without permission in writing from the publisher. The author acknowledges that there are many differences in language translation and have attempted to select a form of Spanish that will be understood in the vast majority of Spanish-speaking situations. For more information and to contact the authors: SpanishChatCompany.com.

ISBN 13: 978-1-946128-10-2

ISBN 10: 1-946128-10-4

Library of Congress Cataloging-in Publication Data on file with publisher.

Published by: Spanish Chat Company
SpanishChatCompany.com

Printed in the United States of America

10 9 8 7 6 5 4 3 2 1

HERE IS WHAT PEOPLE ARE SAYING ABOUT OUR SPANISH CHATBOOK & SPANISH CHATBOOK 2:

"This was the best Spanish learning experience I ever had. The class was extremely upbeat and fun. I will continue using her guides as a reference."

—Tess Snyder Woodmen of the World Insurance

"As a Training Manager for a regional casino, having our Leaders understand basic conversational Spanish is critical to their success in interacting with their teams. Julie does a phenomenal job making the classes interactive."

—Jackie Hansen, Casino Training Manager

"As a tenured educator and facilitator I truly appreciated Julie's ability to flexibly adapt to multiple learning style , two years of studying Spanish was nothing compared to what I learned in two weeks time with Julie. Her philosophy works!" —Spencer K. Terry, Private Consultant

"Spanish Chat with Julie is an experience of enthusiasm for the topic. She is pragmatic, able to teach at the appropriate level and yet challenging in a polite way."

—Dr. Charles Filipi, Professor of Surgery -Creighton

CHEERS FOR OUR ELEMENTARY SPANISH CHATBOOK

"The Spanish Chatbook activities combine lessons on language, history and culture, all wrapped up in an energetic, dynamic presentation. As a principal at a Dual Language school, I have found the Spanish Chatbook classes have helped me communicate more effectively with my students and families. I highly recommend Spanish Chatbooks for everyone!"

Marjorie Schmid, Principal, Crestridge Elementary International Studies & Dual Language Magnet

"When learning to speak a new language, students often feel shy or intimidated when trying to put together more than a few words. Spanish Chat Company's method of teaching Spanish makes the learning process fun and easy, so students show more confidence. I would recommend these beneficial key words and phrases — whether for personal or business use."

—Deb Barelos, Circulation Manager
Omaha Public Library

PRAISE FOR ANOTHER GREAT BOOK BUSINESS SPANISH CHATBOOK:

"The practical and enjoyable lessons were designed to teach our employees to communicate with our Spanish-speaking customers. We learned the language, plus important cultural facts about Spanish-speaking countries."

—Pat Tooles, Corporate Performance
Omaha Public Power District

"I have really enjoyed the *Business Spanish Chatbook*. The pronunciation guides and phrases are valuable tools that I use often in my day-to-day work."

—Jill Regester, Communications Manager
Woodmen of the World Insurance Agency

"The lessons are easy to follow and understand, and the phrases we learned were exactly what we needed to better serve our customers. Julie has that rare gift of making learning fun. She brings such exuberance to her classes, the students learn very easily."

—Terry Wingate, Volunteer Coordinator
Omaha Public Library

OUR CULINARY SPANISH CHATBOOK IS ALSO GETTING RAVE REVIEWS:

"Welcome to the way you will learn Spanish. This is the perspective that should be taken with all languages. Gracias Maestra!"

—Phil Nicols, Culinary student

"Maestra Julia is an engaged and dynamic instructor in the classroom whose passion para el Español y la cocina has also permeated this project."

—Chef Brian O'Malley Academic Director
Institute for the Culinary Arts
Metropolitan Community College

"Culinary Spanish Chatbook is a 'must have' for everyone working in the food industry. There is nothing more frustrating than not being able to communicate with a co-worker. This book is a great tool to help break down those barriers, and it's realistic, upbeat approach makes learning Spanish fun."

—Karen Popp, Operations Manager
WheatFields Eatery and Bakery

SU TAREA = YOUR HOMEWORK

We will use this page to record our homework.

Homework will be checked at the beginning of each class.

PÁGINAS = PAGES	FIRME AQUÍ O PONGA PEGATINES = SIGN HERE OR PUT ON STICKERS
From Lesson 1 Pages 20 & 21 **DUE** _____	
From Lesson 2 Pages 42 & 43 **DUE** _____	
From Lesson 3 Pages 64-66 **DUE** _____	
From Lesson 4 Pages 85 & 86 **DUE** _____	
From Lesson 5 Pages 109 & 110 **DUE** _____	
From Lesson 6 Page 130 **DUE** _____	
ROUGH DRAFT DUE _____	
FINAL PROJECT DUE _____	

ABOUT THE AUTHORS

Julie Jahde Pospishil studied for a semester at the University in San Sebastian, Spain, and has an M.A. in Education-Language Acquisition from the University of Nebraska–Omaha. She has taught Spanish for over 20 years customizing Adult Spanish Classes for Boystown Pediatrics–Bergan Mercy Hospital, Omaha Public Power Development (OPPD), Omaha Public Libraries, Dana College, Woodmen of the World, Casinos, Communications Companies, many banks and Metropolitan Community College. She and Brad own Spanish Chat Company. She loves traveling with her husband, Brad, and has spent summers in 16 different Latin American countries, meeting many amigos. Julie currently teaches classes using her *Spanish Chatbook, Spanish Chatbook 2, Culinary Spanish Chatbook, Business Spanish Chatbook* and *Elementary Spanish Chatbook*. She produces the *Spanish Chatshow* movies and cooks Latin American dishes with her children, Jaden and Elena. She believes "everyone smiles in the same language" and "donde existe voluntad, siempre hay un camino." = "Where there's a will, there's a way."

Brad Pospishil has been a Spanish teacher for the past 18 years at Omaha North Magnet High School. He has a B.A. from Rockhurst University and an M.S. from the University of Wisconsin–Madison in Industrial Relations. He studied Spanish at the University of Nebraska–Lincoln and at ITESM-Querétaro, México. He received his teaching certificate from UNL with endorsements in Spanish, history and government. Brad has traveled extensively in Latin America with his wife, Julie, on "Aventuras con Julia."

CONTENTS

NAME TAG & LIST OF HISPANIC NAMES
SURVEY OF GOALS & NEEDS
INTRODUCTION: A TOUR OF THE BOOK

LESSON 1: READ AND CHAT IN SPANISH IN JUST FIVE MINUTES

- Pronunciation of vowels 1
- Pronunciation of consonants 2
- AEIOU with Introductions of your Spanish Name 3
- Cognates 4
- Using two last names .... 5 & 6
- Accent marks 7
- Greetings and goodbye phrases 8
- Practice: Meet and Greet & Multiple Choice .... 9 & 10
- Tú versus Usted & Making mistakes 11
- Map of Spanish Speaking Countries 12
- Helpful introductory phrases 13
- Matching activity 14
- "Tic-Tac-Toe" game board 15
- Conversational Role Play 16
- Create your own Role Play 17
- Categorizing Hispanics and Latinos 18
- Famous Hispanic-Americans 19
- **TAREA = Homework**: Word Search & Translate Sentences .... 20 & 21
- Audio CD track listing 22
- Desktop Phrase guide 23
- Number Chart 1–9,000 24

LESSON 2: CONNECT AND CHAT

- Review greetings from Lesson 1 25
- Initial contact phrases 26
- Language acquisition—English versus Spanish & Phrases to connect with others 27
- Multiple Choice activity 28
- Differences in Latin American Numbers 29
- "Más o Menos" game 30
- Shopping and pricing phrases 31
- Conversational Role Play & Aztec Calendar 32
- Create your own Role Play 33
- Question words 34
- Information about Spanish Speaking Countries 35
- Spain and Mexico Charts 36
- Trivia about Spain & Mexico 37
- Variations in the Spanish language / Language fluency 38
- Matching activity 39
- "Toma Todo" game 40
- The four ways of saying "the" 41
- **TAREA = Homework**: Crossword puzzle 42
- **TAREA = Homework**: Translate Sentences 43

LESSON 3: CHAT ABOUT THE FAMILY

Review Lessons 1 & 2 & Family members ....44 & 45
Papa vs. Papá & The Mayan number system ....46 & 47
Personal questions and phrases to build rapport 48
Gustar: Expressing likes and dislikes 49
Family Project: Describing your family & Your job & Your age ....50 & 51
Machismo & Hispanic families & Locating Central American countries on a map 52
Central America: Guatemala, El Salvador, Honduras & Nicaragua 53
Central America: Costa Rica & Panama 54
Central American Trivia 55
Phrases about family & Multiple Choice activity 56
Conversational Role Play 57
Alphabet & Piñata game ....58 & 59
Spelling and best wishes phrases & Tongue twisters 60
Final project ideas 61
"Bingo Game Board" and directions ....62 & 63
TAREA = Homework: Matching activity/ 1 phrase puzzle & Translate sentences 64-66

LESSON 4: WHICH WAY TO GO RELAX AND CHAT?

Family presentation 67
International embarkation & disembarkation card 68
Leisure activity phrases, Partner review & Multiple Choice activity ....69 & 70
Adjectives & Colors 71
Phrases for giving and receiving directions & Matching activity ....72 & 73
Introduction to 3 verbs: Tener = to have ....74 & 75
Querer = to want 76
Ir = to go 77
Language connection phrases 78
Conquistadors & Why Spanish is spoken throughout the Americas 79
Conversational Role Play 80
Locating South American countries 81
Colombia, Ecuador, Venezuela & Trivia ....82 & 83
"Around the World" game & Final project evaluation rubric 84
TAREA = Homework: Word Search & Translate Sentences ....85 & 86

LESSON 5: TIME TO SCHEDULE A CHAT

Number practice with "Bingo" 87
Telling time ....88 & 89
Daily routine & Reflexive verbs 90
Tomorrow = Mañana & Tardiness also Holidays & Fiestas 91
Months of the year with a game 92
Days of the week with a mulitple choice activity 93
Weather with charades 94
Calendar phrases to schedule events 95
Practice with schedules & Aztec, Maya & Inca 96
Medical phrases & Body parts with a matching activity 97-99
Bolivia, Perú & Chile 100
Argentina, Uruguay, Paraguay & Trivia ....101 & 102
Conversational Role Play 103
The verbs to be = ser versus estar 104-106
"Which One Is The Lie?" A true/false game and other game ideas ....107 & 108
TAREA = Homework: Crossword puzzle & Translate Sentences ....109 & 110

LESSON 6: CHATTING AT THE RESTAURANT

- Final project presentations & Fiesta 111
- Check for understanding: Trip to Puerto Rico 112
- Menus and Latin American schedules 113
- Restaurant phrases for ordering at the beginning of the meal 114
- Conversational Role Play & Multiple Choice & Phrase puzzle 115-117
- Communication styles 118
- During the meal & End of the meal restaurant phrases 119
- Puerto Rico, Dominican Republic, Cuba & Equatorial Guinea with Trivia .... 120 & 121
- Matching activity 122
- Travel advice 123
- Regular present tense –ar, -er, -ir verb conjugation 124-127
- Conversation starters and "Bingo" game 128
- 10 ideas to continue learning in the future 129
- **TAREA = Homework**: Translate Sentences 130
- Grocery store scavenger hunt and field trip Spanish version .... 131 & 132
- Grocery store scavenger hunt and field trip English version .... 133 & 134

CERTIFICATE OF COMPLETION 135

ANSWER KEY
- For all exercises in Lessons 1–6 137

GLOSSARY
Alphabetical word list of all the phrases in the book
- Spanish to English 153
- English to Spanish 159

BONUS ITEMS / RECIPES
- Travel agent / Final project description 165
- Recipes 166

SUBJECT INDEX 171

GRACIAS / ORDER MORE ONLINE 176

THE PYRAMID OF THE SUN, TEOTIHUACÁN, MÉXICO
IS ONE OF THE LARGEST IN THE WORLD.

LEARN SPANISH TODAY FOR WORK & PLAY

SPANISH CHAT COMPANY

En español me llamo _____
(Spanish name)

My English name is _____

Recorta = Cut out along the dashed lines

NAMES = NOMBRES:

Choose a Spanish first name for yourself and write your new name on the line below. This is the one time in life where you get to choose your own name. Here is a partial list of Hispanic names and a name tag you can use if you are in a class.

WOMEN/LADIES = MUJERES/DAMAS

Adriana	Carolina	Gabriela	Lupe	Paula
Alejandra	Carlota	Gloria	Margarita	Rebeca
Alicia	Cecilia	Graciela	María	Raquel
Alma	Clara	Hilda	Maribel	Rosa
Amalia	Cristina	Inés	Maricarmen	Sandra
Ana	Diana	Isabel	Maricela	Sara
Andrea	Dora	Juana	Marisol	Sofía
Ángela	Elena	Julia	Marta	Susana
Beatriz	Esmeralda	Laura	Mercedes	Teresa
Blanca	Ester	Liliana	Mónica	Victoria
Carmen	Eva	Linda	Olga	Yolanda

MEN/GENTLEMEN = HOMBRES/CABALLEROS

Adán	César	Francisco	Juan	Pedro
Alberto	Daniel	Gonzalo	Julio	Rafael
Alejandro	David	Gregorio	Luis	Ramón
Alfonso	Diego	Guillermo	Manuel	Raúl
Alfredo	Eduardo	Héctor	Marcos	Roberto
Andrés	Emilio	Jaime	Mario	Rubén
Antonio	Enrique	Javier	Mateo	Samuel
Arturo	Ernesto	Jesús	Miguel	Santiago
Benito	Felipe	Joaquín	Nicolás	Timoteo
Bernardo	Félix	Jorge	Oscar	Tomás
Carlos	Fernando	José	Pablo	Victor

WELCOME! = ¡BIENVENIDOS!

This survey will help you identify your goals and needs in order to create the best learning environment possible. Fill out this form and then discuss your answers with a partner or as a group.

Learning requires interest.

1. Why are you interested in learning Spanish? _____
   _____
   _____

Your background affects learning.

2. Have you ever taken a foreign language class? If so, where?
   How many years? _____
   _____
   _____

3. How would you rate your Spanish abilities? Mark the choice that best fits your current level.

   🌎 **I understand Spanish.**
   ☐ Everything
   ☐ Most conversations
   ☐ Some
   ☐ A little
   ☐ Nada =Nothing

   🌎 **I read in Spanish.**
   ☐ Easily without a dictionary to look up words
   ☐ Sporadically, with a dictionary to look up words
   ☐ Nunca = Never

   🌎 **I speak in Spanish.**
   ☐ Fluently
   ☐ With some mistakes
   ☐ Lots of mistakes
   ☐ Nunca = Never

   🌎 **I write in Spanish.**
   ☐ Well, with very few mistakes
   ☐ With some mistakes
   ☐ Lots of mistakes
   ☐ Nunca = Never

Please continue this survey on the next page.

SURVEY OF GOALS & NEEDS

You learn from your problems.

4. Describe a past experience where it would have been helpful to know Spanish.
   _____
   _____
   _____

"Practice makes perfect."

5. How do you plan to study Spanish outside of class? _____
   _____
   _____
   _____
   _____

6. How much time do you expect to practice Spanish each week?_____
   _____
   _____
   _____

You learn better in a positive and respectful environment.

7. What will you do to make learning Spanish a positive experience?_____
   _____
   _____
   _____

8. ¿¿¿Any other comments or questions???_____
   _____
   _____
   _____

9. If you are in a group, these are the first pages that you will tear out of your *Spanish Chatbook* conversational workbook. Please hand it to your teacher or group leader and add the following information:

Name = Nombre: _____

Email = Correo electrónico: _____

Phone number = Número de teléfono: _____

Introduction: A Tour of the Book

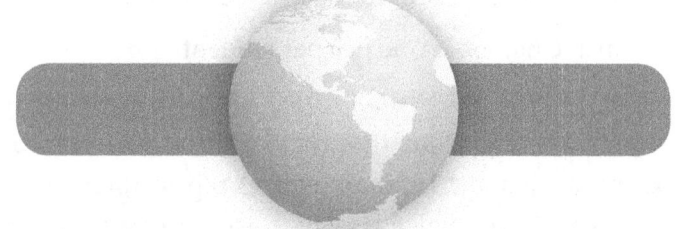

Welcome! = ¡Bienvenidos!

We are so glad you have joined this learning adventure, and we hope you will be able to use these phrases immediately. This book has useful, practical phrases designed to help anyone communicate with Hispanic friends and clients. If you have forgotten your high school Spanish, and you really need to communicate, then this is the book for you.

Spanish Chatbook will help you speak in real-world Spanish right now. Each of the six lessons includes 12–15 conversational phrases. The first time a phrase is introduced, it will have the English phrase = the Spanish phrase followed by the pronunciation guide in italics. This guide is meant to help a native English speaker read the Spanish phrase out loud and pronounce the words correctly.

Each new word in the pronunciation guide is capitalized. For example, nice to meet you = mucho gusto (*Moo-cho Goose-toh*). Two vowels are sometimes combined as indicated by a slash: Bien = (*Bee/ehn*). A word with an accent mark means that the syllable is stressed and should be emphasized when spoken. For example, telephone = teléfono (*Teh-LEH-foh-noh*) indicates to put the emphasis on the "*LEH.*"

Many native speakers will have a variety of ways to say the same sentence, such as "How are you?", "How are you doing?", "How is it going?" and "What's up?" None of the ways are wrong. They are just, different styles. In this *Spanish Chatbook*, we have chosen a phrase and will review that same phrase over and over. Feel free to change and customize it to fit the slang of your Hispanic friends. We've tried to use correct Spanish without being too formal or too "Spanglish."

INTRODUCTION: A TOUR OF THE BOOK

USTED NECESITA = YOU NEED:

1. **Tijeras** = Scissors: one per student to cut out the flashcards
2. **Sobre** = Envelope: one per student to keep the flashcards together
3. **Dados** = Dice: one per every 2-3 students for some of the games
4. **Instrumentos** = Instruments: one per student, if possible or one shaker to pass around the group during the activity in Lesson 1 #3.
5. **Pedazos** = Pieces: 16 small squares or dried beans for Bingo
6. **Libros** = Spanish Chatbook: one per per student
7. **Audio** = Use *Spanish Chatbook Audio tracks* together with the book to maximize your learning.. On the audio tracks, native speakers pronounce the Spanish phrases, allow time for you to repeat them, and act out each of the phrases in conversational role plays. Listen to over 75 phrases and typical conversations while driving, working, or exercising.
8. **Música Latina** = Latin Music: to play at the beginning of each lesson.
9. **Recetas** = Recipes: You may want to have students sign up to bring a Hispanic appetizer and healthy snacks during each class. Use recipes from pages 166-170.
10. **Paciencia** = Patience: Stay positive, stick to the lessons, tell students you will answer other questions before or after each session. Keep smiling!

EL LIBRO = THE BOOK:

Each lesson will take about 1-2 hours to complete and contains a review of the phrases from the previous lesson, 12-15 new phrases, spoken practice, multiple choice exercises, matching, a skit with a typical conversation, grammar tidbits, translation practice, an exam, flashcards, games and puzzles. Awareness of the Hispanic culture is woven into each lesson with facts about each Spanish-speaking country, trivia questions, an explanation of cultural differences in styles and overall cultural diversity considerations. Find a friend, family member, lunch study group or native speaker to help you with the partner activities.

This book, Spanish Chatbook 2 & Business Spanish Chatbook all use the formal style. written in the polite "usted" form, most commonly spoken among adult acquaintances and used for customer service. "Usted" is pronounced Oos-tehd—like the oo in the word moon. Our Culinary Spanish Chatbook and Elementary Spanish Chatbook are written in the informal "tú" form. Find out more information at our website, SpanishChatCompany.com.

READ AND CHAT IN SPANISH IN JUST FIVE MINUTES

GOALS: In this lesson you will learn about these topics: pronunciation of vowels and consonants, how to learn to read and chat in Spanish in five minutes, common greetings and goodbye phrases, using two last names, tú versus usted, accent marks, helpful introductory phrases and categorizing Hispanics and Latinos and famous Hispanic-Americans.

LESSON 1: READ AND CHAT IN SPANISH IN JUST FIVE MINUTES

1 = UNO

YOU CAN LEARN TO READ SPANISH IN FIVE MINUTES

This guide will help you pronounce and read every word in Spanish, although you will have to use detective skills to be able to understand anything. Read these words and phrases out loud, paying careful attention to the sounds of each letter.

THE VOWELS = LAS VOCALES:

The good news is, the vowels are always the same!

A *(ah)*   la banana *(Lah Bah-nah-nah)* = the banana
la mamá *(Lah Mah-MAH)* = the mom

E *(eh)*   las escaleras *(Lahs Ehs-cah-leh-rahs)* = the stairs
el bebé *(Ehl Beh-BEH)* = the baby

I *(eee)*   sí *(SEE)* = yes
qui-qui-ri-quí *(Kee-kee-ree-KEE)* = cock-a-doodle-doo

O *(oh)*   no *(Noh)* = no
¿Cómo? *(KOH-moh)* = How's that?

U *(oo)* as in moon   Mucho gusto. *(Moo-cho Goose-toh)* = Nice to meet you.

Note: When a strong vowel, (A, E, O) is combined with a weak vowel, (I, U) it makes a diphthong. When spoken, the two vowels are slurred together into the same syllable. In this book, you will see diphthongs with a slash mark, for example; ¿Tiene tiempo? *(Tee/ehn-neh Tee/ehm-poh?)* = Do you have time? Sometimes accent marks/tildes are used to break up the two syllables and override the diphthong rule. For example, el día *(dee-ah)* = the day. Listen to the native speakers on the *Spanish Chatbook* audio tracks to help you.

2 = DOS

THE CONSONANTS = LAS CONSONANTES

B & V sound similar   ¡Vámonos! *(VAH-moh-nohs)* = Let's go!

H is silent   Hola. *(Oh-lah)* = Hello
(Cross it out)   Habla *(Ah-blah)* = talk

J & GE & GI   Julia *(Who-lee/ah)* = Julie
soft sound like H   José *(Ho-SEH)* = Joe
    gerente *(Heh-wren-teh)* = manager
    girasol *(Hee-rah-sohl)* = sunflower

GA, GO, GU
are a hard G   gato *(Gah-toh)* = cat
some have umlauts   bilingüe *(Bee-leen-goo/eh)* = bilingual

QUE (keh)   ¿Por qué? *(Pohr KEH)* = Why?
    porque *(Pohr-keh)* = because

QUI (kee)   ¿Quién? *(Kee-ehn)* = Who?

LL (yeah OR yah)   Me llamo _____.
    (Meh Yah-moh) = My name is_____.

Ñ as in bunion   Señor/Sr. *(Seh-ñyour)* = Mr. or Sir
    Señora/Sra. *(Seh-ñyour-ah)* = Mrs. or Ma'am
    Señorita/Srta. *(Seh-ñyour-ree-tah)* = Miss (younger)

RR is never at the beginning of a word and it is trilled/rolled:
    Correcto *(Koh-rrehk-toh)* = correct
    Perro *(Peh-rroh)* = dog
    Without rolling the r it would be: Pero *(Peh-roh)* = but

---

Having trouble rolling your RR's? Your tongue muscle needs exercise. You should be able to roll your RR's if you spend a few months practicing this Spanish phrase:

Un tigre, dos tigres, tres tigres = One tiger, two tigers, three tigers
(Oon Tee-greh, Dohs Tee-grehs, Trehs Tee-grehs)

LESSON 1: READ AND CHAT IN SPANISH IN JUST FIVE MINUTES

3 = TRES

Practice this chant using rainsticks, maracas, drums, or some other instrument to provide rhythm: **"A, E, I, O, U, ¿Cómo se llama usted?** *(Ah, Eh, Eee, Oh, Ooh, KOH-moh Seh Yah-mah Oos-tehd?)* = A, E, I, O, U, What is your name?

At the end of the chant you say, **"me llamo _____."** *(Meh Yah-moh)* meaning, "my name is _____." Everyone else says, **"mucho gusto."** *(Moo-cho Goose-toh.)* which means, "nice to meet you." If you have a group, play "hot potato" with a maraca. The person holding the maraca at the end of the chant says, **"me llamo _____."** The group then replies, **"mucho gusto."**

Note: "Me llamo..." literally means, "I call myself..." Please do NOT mistakenly say, "Me llamo es..." which means "I call myself is...." However you can say, "Mi nombre es..." which is a slightly more formal version of "My name is..."

The authentic original rhyme in Latin America is, "A, E, I, O, U, un burro sabe más que tú," meaning "A, E, I, O, U, a donkey knows more than you." Remember back to when you or your child was learning to speak English. They started out with wha-wha for water and everyone cheered. We will work together as we take baby steps to learn this new language.

4 = CUATRO

There are some Spanish words that resemble English words. English and Spanish are both Latin-based languages and some words are similar. Read these words out loud using your new pronunciation skills and then guess the meaning of each word. When you are finished, refer to the Answer Key at the back of the book.

1. banco = _____
2. refrigerador = _____
3. café = _____
4. teléfono = _____
5. restaurante = _____
6. coliflor = _____

5 = CINCO

In many Hispanic countries, people use two last names every day. You would use both last names when looking up someone in the phone book. There are even two blanks on most official government and school forms. This may cause confusion when dealing with human resources issues. Be aware that the father's last name, is always listed first, followed by the mother's last name. In other words, it is your paternal grandfather's last name followed by your maternal grandfather's last name. Confused? Look at the examples below.

Example: José Ramírez García marries María Cruz Vásquez. (See the following family tree.) Their son is named José Carlos Ramírez Cruz and their daughter is María Carmen Ramírez Cruz. A woman getting married may keep both her maiden names or add de _____ with her husband's last name. For example, if the daughter, María Carmen Ramírez Cruz, marries Luis Perez Morales, she may be María Carmen Ramírez Cruz de Perez or she may drop Cruz and be María Carmen Ramírez Perez.

In the United States, the son may shorten his name to Carlos Ramirez (dropping José and Cruz and also dropping the accent mark/tilde). He may choose to hyphenate his last name as Ramírez-Cruz. José Carlos may even be called Carlitos as a child. The daughter may be called Carmen Ramírez or even Carmen Perez. In many Latin American countries, children take pride in reciting not only their two last names, but adding on the names of more generations. Nicknames and using the endings of –ito and –ita is common throughout the Hispanic world. Instead of calling a co-worker "amigo", it would create better rapport if you would use the co-worker's name.

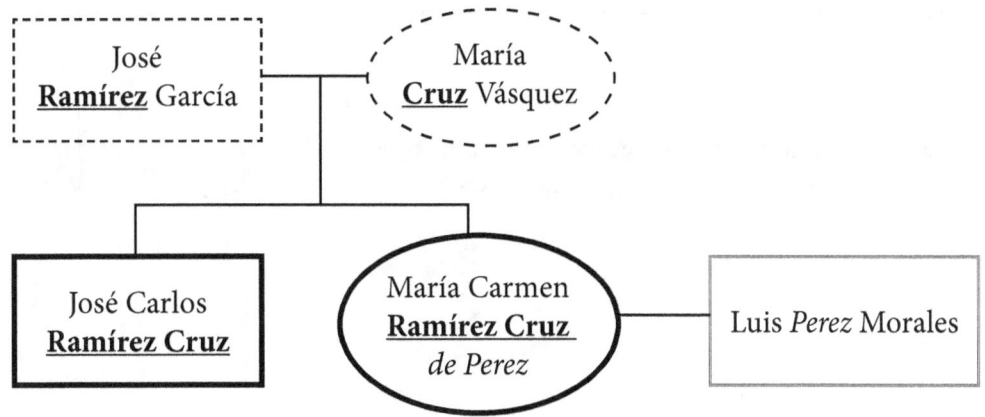

6 = SEIS

What would your Hispanic name look like? Try it out using the example below. Then ask a Hispanic friend if they ever use two last names.

For example, what was your father's last name? _____+

What was your mother's maiden name? _____ +

(For women only) de _____ (your husband's last name).

If you lived in a Spanish-speaking country, there would be space for these multiple names on most official forms and documents.

7 = SIETE

Do you need an accent = tilde? Here are some computer keyboard shortcuts. Another method is to go to insert and select symbols. Note: check online help for more options if this doesn't work for your computer. For more Spanish marks and how and when to use an accent, see our next book, *Spanish Chatbook 2*.

ON A PC: For á, é, í, ó, ú, Á, É, Í, Ó, Ú

Hold down CTRL and '(apostrophe) at the same time; then the next letter you type will have an accent mark.
If this does not work then search online for other techniques.

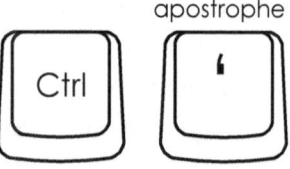

___

ON A MAC: For á, é, í, ó, ú, Á, É, Í, Ó, Ú

Hold down both the option and e keys at the same time; then the next letter you type will have an accent.

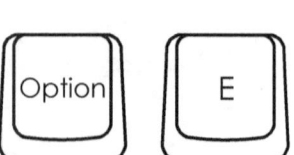

LESSON 1: READ AND CHAT IN SPANISH IN JUST FIVE MINUTES

8 = OCHO

Let's begin chatting with these common phrases for greetings and good-byes. Read the phrase out loud using the italics to help you with pronunciation.

1. Good morning. =
   Buenos días.
   (Bweh-nohs DEE-ahs.)

2. Good afternoon. Good evening. (12 p.m. – dark) =
   Buenas tardes.
   (Bweh-nahs Tahr-dehs.)

3. Good night. =
   Buenas noches.
   (Bweh-nahs Noh-chehs.)

4. See you later. =
   Hasta luego.
   (Ahs-tah Loo/eh-goh.)

9 = NUEVE

Find a Spanish-speaker and practice saying the appropriate greeting for the corresponding time of day. If you are working in a group, greet as many people as possible in the next 3 minutes.

#1 says "Buenos Días. Buenas tardes. Buenas noches."

#2 says "Buenos Días. Buenas tardes. Buenas noches."

#1 says "Me llamo _____. = My name is ...
   (Meh Yah-moh ...)

#1 says "Me llamo _____. = My name is ...
   (Meh Yah-moh ...)

#1 and #2 Both Finish with, "Hasta luego."

Now find someone else to greet in Spanish.

10 = DIEZ

Circle the English choice that matches the Spanish phrase.

1. Buenos días.
   a. Good afternoon.
   b. Good night.
   c. Good morning.
   d. Good job.

2. Hasta luego.
   a. Goodbye.
   b. See you later.
   c. Never again.
   d. See you soon.

3. Buenas noches.
   a. Good afternoon.
   b. Good night.
   c. Good morning.
   d. Good nachos.

4. Buenas tardes.
   a. Good afternoon.
   b. Good night.
   c. Good morning.
   d. Good tacos.

11 = ONCE

Tú versus usted (abbreviation Ud.) both words mean YOU in Latin America. Tú *(TOO)* is the casual and informal you versus usted (*Oos-tehd* like the oo in moon), which is the polite and formal way of saying you. Usted is used as respect for customer service, courtesy, anyone older, or higher ranking. Use usted for an initial meeting. We will use the usted form because it is best for adult acquaintances. Tú is used with family members and close friends in your same age group. For more information on using the tú form, we recommend our books, *Culinary Spanish Chatbook* and the *Elementary Spanish Chatbook*.

One company had complaints with a customer service representative who was always addressing clients in the informal tú form. Her evaluations were lower, due to this informality. If you are in doubt in a social situation, just ask, "Is it okay to use the tú form?" = "¿Me puede tutear?" For more than one person use ustedes *(Uds.)* = Y'all or all of you. In Spain, Vosotros is used instead of ustedes.

Have you ever made a mistake? One funny example of a communication blunder happened in Spain, when the author pointed to some garlic cloves = ajo and accidentally said, "ojo" which means "eyeball." The shopkeeper thought it was so funny that he went over to the fish counter and got a fresh "ojo" and handed it to her with a big smile = sonrisa. Learn to laugh and cheer at your mistakes or mishaps because that means you are at least trying. In fact, many native speakers enjoy having fun with the language.

LESSON 1: READ AND CHAT IN SPANISH IN JUST FIVE MINUTES

12 = DOCE
Map containing the Spanish-speaking countries

This map highlights the 21 Spanish-speaking countries. Starting on the left of the front cover, here are the names corresponding to the flags of each country: Argentina, Bolivia, Chile, Nicaragua, Panama, Paraguay, Colombia, Uruguay, Venezuela, Mexico, Guatemala, Peru, Spain, El Salvador, Dominican Republic, Costa Rica, Cuba, Ecuador, Puerto Rico, Honduras, Equatorial Guinea.

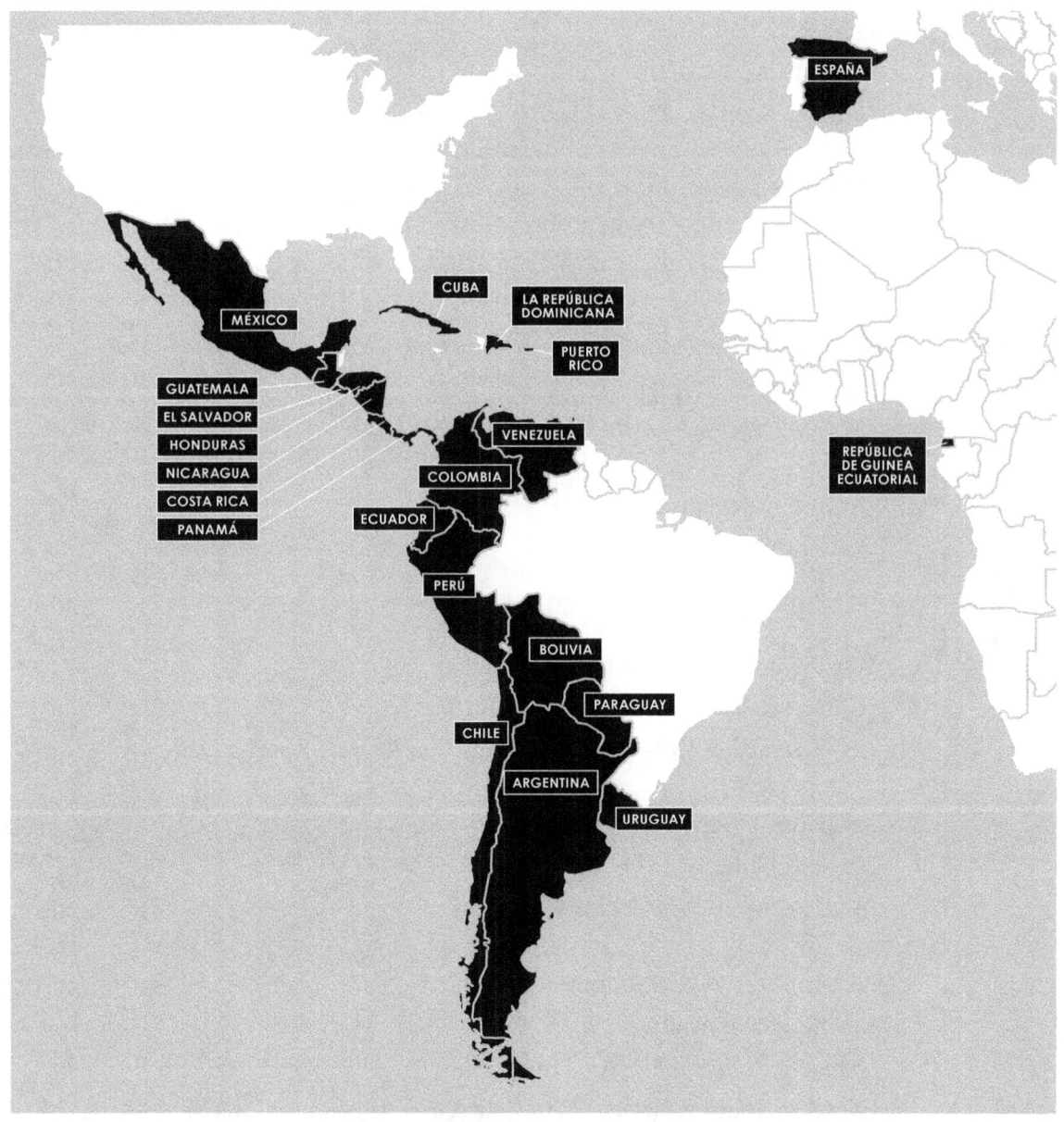

LESSON 1: READ AND CHAT IN SPANISH IN JUST FIVE MINUTES

13 = TRECE

Use these eight helpful introductory phrases to take control of the conversation and slow down the speaker. Working with a partner, have one person ask the question and the partner answer in Spanish.

1. Hello. How are you? =
   Hola. ¿Cómo está usted?
   (Oh-lah, KOH-moh Ehs-TAH Oos-tehd?)

2. I am fine. And you? =
   Estoy bien. ¿Y usted?
   (Ehs-toy Bee/ehn. Ee Oos-tehd?)

3. How may I help you? =
   ¿En qué le puedo ayudar?
   (Ehn KEH Leh Pweh-doh Ah-you-dahr?)

4. Slow down. Repeat that. =
   Más despacio. Repítalo.
   (MAHS Dehs-pah-see/oh.) (Reh-PEE-tah-loh.)

5. Do you understand? =
   ¿Entiende?
   (¿Ehn-tee/ehn-deh?)

6. What is your name? Your last name? =
   ¿Cómo se llama usted? ¿Su apellido?
   (KOH-moh Seh Yah-mah Oos-tehd?) (Soo Ah-peh-yee-doh?)

7. My name is Julie. =
   Me llamo Julia.
   (Meh Yah-moh Who-lee/ah.)

8. Nice to meet you. Goodbye. =
   Mucho gusto. Adiós.
   (Moo-cho Goose-toh.) (Ah-dee/OHS!)
   (Note: In South America "Chau" or "Ciao" is used for "bye.")

SPANISH CHATBOOK ❶ © SPANISH CHAT COMPANY

14 = CATORCE

Write the letter of the corresponding English phrase on the line next to the Spanish phrase.

1.	_____ ¿Cómo se llama usted?	A. *(ah)*		Do you understand?
2.	_____ Repítalo.	B. *(beh)*		See you later.
3.	_____ Hasta luego.	C. *(seh)*		Hello.
4.	_____ ¿En qué le puedo ayudar?	D. *(deh)*		Slow down.
5.	_____ Buenas noches.	E. *(eh)*		Repeat that.
6.	_____ Estoy bien.	F. *(ehf-feh)*		And you?
7.	_____ Hola.	G. *(heh)*		What is your name?
8.	_____ Me llamo Julia.	H. *(ah-cheh)*		Goodbye!
9.	_____ Más despacio.	I. *(eeee)*		Nice to meet you.
10.	_____ ¡Adiós!	J. *(hoh-tah)*		Good morning.
11.	_____ ¿Y usted?	K. *(kah)*		My name is Julie.
12.	_____ Mucho gusto.	L. *(ehl-leh)*		How may I help you?
13.	_____ Buenas tardes.	M. *(ehm-meh)*		I am fine.
14.	_____ ¿Entiende?	N. *(ehn-neh)*		Good night.
15.	_____ Buenos días.	Ñ. *(ehn--ñyeh)*		How are you?
16.	_____ ¿Cómo está usted?	O. *(oh)*		Good afternoon.

15 = QUINCE

To play this "Tic-Tac-Toe" game, you and your partner will share one board depicted here. Cut out the X and O pieces and the flashcards found on the next page. Put nine flashcards, Spanish-side up on the board. Player X will go first, choosing a square that will help to get three in a row. Player X will read the Spanish for that square and say what it means in English in order to cover it up with an X piece. Then it is Player O's turn. Player O will read the Spanish for the square and say what it means in English. Play until someone gets three in row, "Tres en Raya" or "Tic-Tac-Toe." To make it more difficult, put the English-side up and say the answer in Spanish. ¡Buena suerte! = Good luck!

"Three-in-a-Row = Tres en Raya" game board

CUT OUT THE GAME PIECES FROM THE FLASHCARD ON THE NEXT PAGE

LESSON 1: READ AND CHAT IN SPANISH IN JUST FIVE MINUTES

Cut these flashcards apart and save them in an envelope to use during the games in this book. Cut out the X's and O's for this game. Strive to find at least five minutes each day to review them.

Cut out the X & O pieces on the side of this page!

Hello. How are you?	Good morning.	Good afternoon/ evening.
LESSON 1	LESSON 1	LESSON 1
Good night.	See you later.	Nice to meet you. Goodbye!
LESSON 1	LESSON 1	LESSON 1
My name is Julie.	I am fine. And you?	How may I help you?
LESSON 1	LESSON 1	LESSON 1
What is your name?	Slow down. Repeat that.	Do you understand?
LESSON 1	LESSON 1	LESSON 1

O
O
O
O
O
X
X
X
X
X

© SPANISH CHAT COMPANY   SPANISH CHATBOOK ❶

LESSON 1: READ AND CHAT IN SPANISH IN JUST FIVE MINUTES

Buenas tardes. *(Bweh-nahs Tahr-dehs.)*	Buenos días. *(Bweh-nohs DEE-ahs.)*	Hola. *(Oh-lah.)* ¿Cómo está usted? *(KOH-moh Ehs-TAH Oos-tehd?)*
Mucho gusto. *(Moo-cho Goose-toh.)* ¡Adiós! *(Ah-dee/OHS!)*	Hasta luego. *(Ahs-tah Loo/eh-goh.)*	Buenas noches. *(Bweh-nahs Noh-chehs.)*
¿En qué le puedo ayudar? *(Ehn KEH Leh Pweh-doh Ah-you-dahr?)*	Estoy bien. *(Ehs-toy Bee/ehn.)* ¿Y usted? *(Ee Oos-tehd?)*	Me llamo Julia. *(Meh Yah-moh Who-lee/ah.)*
¿Entiende? *(Ehn-tee/ehn-deh?)*	Más despacio. *(MAHS Dehs-pah-see/oh.)* Repítalo. *(Reh-PEE-tah-loh.)*	¿Cómo se llama usted? *(KOH-moh Seh Yah-mah Oos-tehd?)*

LESSON 1: READ AND CHAT IN SPANISH IN JUST FIVE MINUTES

16 = DIECISÉIS

Have one person say the lines for María and the other person say the lines for José, replacing María and José with your new Spanish names. Then switch roles. If you have a group, have two people present this as a skit.

María:	¡Hola!
José:	Buenas tardes.
María:	Buenas tardes. ¿Cómo está usted?
José:	Estoy bien, gracias. ¿Y usted?
María:	No estoy bien. Estoy muy mal. ¿Cómo se llama?
	(muy mal= very bad)
José:	Me llamo José. ¿Y usted?
María:	Me llamo María. Mucho gusto.
José:	Mucho gusto. Hasta luego.
María:	Hasta luego.

17 = DIECISIETE

Fill in the following blanks to write your own skit. Refer to 14 = catorce for help. If you have a group, present these to each other.

Estudiante #1	¡Hola!
Estudiante #2	Buenos días. Buenas tardes. Buenas noches. (Circle one that fits now)
Estudiante #1	Buenos días. Buenas tardes. Buenas noches. (Circle one that fits now) ¿Cómo está usted?
Estudiante #2	Estoy _____ gracias. ¿Y usted? (Bien, mal)
Estudiante #1	Estoy _____. ¿Cómo se llama usted? (Bien, mal)
Estudiante #2	Me llamo _____. (Your Spanish name). ¿Y usted?
Estudiante #1	Me llamo _____. Mucho gusto.
Estudiante #2	Mucho gusto. Hasta luego.
Estudiante #1	Hasta luego.

18 = DIECIOCHO

Latina? Hispanic? Chicano? Mexican? Which one should you use? What is the correct term?

- Spanish is the language. Please don't call someone a "Spanish" person.

- Spanish speakers are any persons who speak Spanish regardless of race. ¡Felicidades! = Congratulations! You are now a Spanish speaker.

- Latinos are people from Latin America (Central and South America) not usually including Spain. Latino or Latina is used often in the media and for cultural events.

- Spaniards are people from Spain.

- Mexicans are people who were born in México.

- Chicanos and Mexican-Americans are U.S. citizens of Mexican descent.

- Guatemalans are people who were born in Guatemala or born to Guatemalan parents. This pattern would continue with every Spanish-speaking country represented.

- The United States of America in Spanish is "Los Estados Unidos de América," also abbreviated with EE.UU. Therefore, a United States citizen is known as "estadounidense." You would probably be understood if you said you were an "americano" or "norte americano," but the terms aren't entirely accurate. All the people in North, South and Central America are also Americans. North America includes the countries of Canada, México and the United States.

- The slang terms of güera or gringo or yanqui are sometimes used to refer to U.S. citizens. These may have negative connotations depending on context.

19 = DIECINUEVE

- Hispanics are people from the countries formerly ruled by Spain. The majority of Hispanics speak the Spanish language. The term Hispanic is used by the government to describe people from Spanish-speaking countries. Each of the following lessons will include cultural information about these Hispanic countries.

- Hispanic-Americans are U.S. citizens of Hispanic descent. Hispanic-Americans have made significant contributions to the United States history and culture and continue to influence many lives. Hispanics comprise 17% of the overall U.S. population with almost 50% in some States. A few influential people include César Chávez (labor leader), Gloria Estefan (singer), Alex Rodriguez (baseball player), Sonia Sotomayor and Elena Kagan (Supreme Court Justices), Rita Moreno (actress), Tito Puente (drummer) and many more.

- Hispanic Heritage Month: September 15–October 15 is the time to celebrate Hispanic culture and achievements of Hispanic Americans. México, Guatemala, El Salvador, Honduras, Nicaragua, Costa Rica and Chile all celebrate their independence days on either September 15, 16 or 18. During Hispanic Heritage Month you could post pictures of your Hispanic employees or make a display highlighting the contributions of famous Hispanics. Check for local events celebrating the Hispanic culture. Send the dates and times to staff members to encourage participation.

- Hispanics also are known for their slang. Some Spanish-speaking individuals may say the phrases differently from what you are learning in this book. Our best advice is to learn these phrases as a foundation and then expand and build your vocabulary. For example, you will hear some very casual phrases in conversations especially among family members and close friends. You may hear, "Hey, how are ya?" = "¿Oye, qué tál?" *(Oh-yeh, KEH Tahl?)* or "What's up?" = "¿Qué pasa?" *(KEH Pah-sah?)* You can respond by saying, "Nothing." = "Nada." *(Nah-dah.)*

- If you have friends or acquaintances = compañeras that speak Spanish, you may have heard a few bad words. Most people seem to be able to learn those very quickly and remember them on their own, so we will focus on "clean Spanish" in this book.

20 = VEINTE

Now you have an opportunity to practice. Complete exercises 20 = veinte and 21 = and then check your answers in the Answer Key. Find these Spanish words in the word search and then write the English on the line next to each word. The Spanish words are from the phrases in 13 = trece. ¡Buena suerte! = Good luck!

A	O	D	E	S	P	A	C	I	O	L	M	S	I	P
V	D	S	M	R	T	S	A	Y	U	D	A	R	E	S
R	D	Í	A	S	M	X	T	O	Y	Z	B	S	Á	R
I	M	I	S	G	Á	C	D	G	Á	V	E	M	O	S
R	E	P	Í	T	A	L	O	H	I	S	S	J	K	E
T	P	D	M	L	B	R	A	D	T	M	T	Ñ	O	D
J	Í	S	U	P	Q	U	V	Á	W	Y	A	Z	E	N
S	N	V	C	Ó	M	O	S	N	O	R	R	J	L	E
E	E	C	H	T	L	A	B	R	O	M	D	N	E	I
L	I	O	O	L	M	F	O	V	R	A	E	N	N	T
L	B	J	H	U	L	P	A	Í	S	D	M	O	A	N
A	R	A	Í	G	W	F	L	N	M	U	S	C	P	E
M	B	D	D	E	R	U	A	N	I	T	O	H	X	V
A	E	E	N	O	T	S	U	G	L	P	M	E	C	R
S	A	N	P	U	S	T	E	D	J	U	L	I	A	X

Word search = Buscapalabras

CÓMO _____   TARDE _____

ESTÁ _____   MUCHO _____

DÍA _____   GUSTO _____

NOCHE _____   DESPACIO _____

AYUDAR _____   REPÍTALO _____

ENTIENDE _____   POR FAVOR _____

BIEN _____   USTED _____

MÁS _____   SE LLAMA _____

21 = VEINTIUNO

Translate these phrases. Write the English for the first eight phrases and write the Spanish for the last eight phrases. This may be done as an exam or as homework for the next lesson. When finished check your answers in the Answer Key.

1. Hola. _____
2. ¿Y usted? _____
3. Buenos días. _____
4. ¡Adiós! _____
5. Estoy bien. _____
6. ¿Entiende? _____
7. Más despacio. _____
8. Buenas noches. _____
9. What is your name? _____
10. Repeat that. _____
11. Good afternoon. _____
12. See you later. _____
13. How may I help you? _____
14. Nice to meet you. _____
15. How are you? _____
16. My name is Julie. _____

LESSON 1: READ AND CHAT IN SPANISH IN JUST FIVE MINUTES

22 = VEINTIDÓS

Need a native speaker to pronounce the phrases?
Wish you could practice in the car or while exercising?
Would you like to reinforce what you've learned?
Want to hear these Spanish words pronounced correctly?

Our *Spanish Chatbook* CD/Audio guide is now available. Enjoy listening to over 75 useful phrases and conversational role plays designed specifically to improve communication. Each time you see the Audio symbol in the book, you will be able to follow along to enhance your Spanish skills. Native speakers pronounce the Spanish phrases, allow time for you to repeat them, and act out each of the conversational role plays. Listen to these 75+ phrases and typical conversations while driving, working, or exercising. Pair the book and audio together to maximize your learning experience! Order the CD/Audio from our website, SpanishChatCompany.com.

SPANISH CHATBOOK AUDIO TRACKS

1. **Introduction to** *Spanish Chatbook* **CD/Audio**
2. Lesson 1 *#8* **Common greetings & goodbyes**
3. Lesson 1 *#13* **Helpful introductory phrases**
4. Lesson 1 *#16* **A conversational role play**
5. Lesson 2 *#26* **Initial contact phrases**
6. Lesson 2 *#27* **Phrases to connect with others**
7. Lesson 2 *#31* **Shopping and pricing phrases**
8. Lesson 2 *#32* **A conversational role play**
9. Lesson 2 *#33* **Now create your own conversational role play**
10. Lesson 3 *#48* **Personal questions and phrases to build rapport**
11. Lesson 3 *#56* **Phrases about family**
12. Lesson 3 *#57* **A conversational role play**
13. Lesson 3 *#60* **Spelling and best wishes phrases**
14. Lesson 3 *#60* **Tongue twisters – Pepe**
15. Lesson 3 *#60* **Tongue twisters – Guitarra**
16. Lesson 3 *#60* **Tongue twisters – Compadre**
17. Lesson 3 *#60* **Tongue twisters – Tristes tigres**
18. Lesson 4 *#69* **Leisure activity phrases**
19. Lesson 4 *#72* **Giving and receiving directions**
20. Lesson 4 *#78* **Language connection phrases**
21. Lesson 4 *#80* **A conversational role play**
22. Lesson 5 *#95* **Calendar phrases to schedule events**
23. Lesson 5 *#97* **Medical phrases**
24. Lesson 5 *#103* **A conversational role play**
25. Lesson 6 *#114* **Restaurant ordering and beginning of the meal phrases**
26. Lesson 6 *#115* **A conversational role play**
27. Lesson 6 *#119* **During and end of the meal restaurant phrases**
28. **Thank you and Final credits**

LESSON 1: READ AND CHAT IN SPANISH IN JUST FIVE MINUTES

23 = VEINTITRÉS

Post this somewhere handy to help you in Spanish-speaking situations.
Fill in the five blank rows with useful phrases from the other lessons.

GOOD MORNING. = BUENOS DÍAS. *(Bweh-nohs DEE-ahs.)*
GOOD AFTERNOON. GOOD EVENING. = BUENAS TARDES. *(Bweh-nahs Tahr-dehs.)*
MY NAME IS _____. = ME LLAMO _____. *(Meh Yah-moh _____)*
SLOW DOWN. = MÁS DESPACIO. *(MAHS Dehs-pah-see/oh.)*
DO YOU UNDERSTAND? = ¿ENTIENDE? *(Ehn-tee/ehn-deh?)*
REPEAT THAT, PLEASE.= REPÍTALO, POR FAVOR. *(Reh-PEE-tah-loh, Pohr Fah-vohr.)*
HAVE A GREAT DAY. = QUE TENGA UN BUEN DÍA. *(Keh Tehn-gah Oon Bwhen DEE-ah.)*
HOW DO YOU SAY __ IN SPANISH? = ¿CÓMO SE DICE __ EN ESPAÑOL? *(KOH-moh Seh Dee-seh ___ Ehn Eh-spah-ñyohl?)*

© SPANISH CHAT COMPANY

24 = VEINTICUATRO

Find the similarities as you read across the rows of this number chart. Do you notice any patterns? Hang this chart in your office space for quick reference.

LOS NÚMEROS = THE NUMBERS

COUNTING BY 1'S	COUNTING BY 1'S	COUNTING BY 10'S	COUNTING BY 100'S	COUNTING BY 1,000'S
0 cero (Seh-roh) 1 uno (Oo-noh)	11 once (Ohn-seh)	10 diez (Dee/ehs)	100 cien (See/ehn) 110 ciento diez (See/ehn-toh Dee-ehs)	1000 mil (Meel)
2 dos (Dohs)	12 doce (Doh-seh)	20 veinte (Veh/een-teh)	200 doscientos (Doh-see/ehn-tohs)	2018 dos mil dieciocho (Dee/eh-see/oh-cho)
3 tres (Trehs)	13 trece (Treh-seh)	30 treinta (Treh/een-tah)	300 trescientos (Treh-see/ehn-tohs)	3.000 tres mil (Trehs Meel)
4 cuatro (Coo/ah-troh)	14 catorce (Kah-tohr-seh)	40 cuarenta (Coo/ah-rent-tah)	400 cuatrocientos (Coo/ah-troh-see/ehn-tohs)	4.000 cuatro mil (Coo/ah-troh Meel)
5 cinco (Seen-koh)	15 quince (Keen-seh)	50 cincuenta (Seen-qwehn-tah)	500 quinientos (Kee-nee/ehn-tohs)	5.000 cinco mil (Seen-koh Meel)
6 seis (Seh/ace)	16 dieciséis (Dee/eh-see-SEH/ace)	60 sesenta (Seh-sehn-tah)	600 seiscientos (Seh/ace-see/ehn-tohs)	6.000 seis mil (Seh/ace Meel)
7 siete (See/eh-teh)	17 diecisiete (Dee/eh-see-see/eh-teh)	70 setenta (Seh-tent-tah)	700 setecientos (Seh-teh-see/ehn-tohs)	7.000 siete mil (See/eh-teh Meel)
8 ocho (Oh-cho)	18 dieciocho (Dee/eh-see/oh-cho)	80 ochenta (Oh-chen-tah)	800 ochocientos (Oh-cho-see/ehn-tohs)	8.000 ocho mil (Oh-cho Meel)
9 nueve (Noo/eh-veh) 10 diez (Dee/ehs)	19 diecinueve (Dee/eh-see-noo/eh-veh)	90 noventa (Noh-vehnt-tah)	900 novecientos (Noh-veh-see/ehn-tohs)	9.000 nueve mil (Noo/eh-veh Meel)

CONNECT AND CHAT

GOALS: In this lesson you will learn about these topics: initial contact, language acquisition; English vs. Spanish, connecting with others, numbers 1–9,000, shopping and prices, question words, Spain, Mexico, variations in the Spanish language and the four ways of saying "the."

LESSON 2: CONNECT AND CHAT

25 = VEINTICINCO

Begin by reviewing some of the phrases from Lesson 1. Fill in the missing Spanish word. Then take turns reading them aloud. Remember to use A, E, I, O, U to pronounce the phrases correctly.

1. Buenos _____
2. ¿Y _____ ?
3. ¿Cómo _____ ?
4. Estoy _____ .
5. Mucho _____ .
6. ¿En qué le puedo _____ ?
7. Hasta _____ .

26 = VEINTISÉIS

Practice these three phrases that will help with initial contact when someone speaks only in Spanish. Use the pronunciation in italics to guide you.

1. Please wait one moment. =
   Espere un momento, por favor.
   (Ehs-peh-reh Oon Moh-mehn-toh, Pohr Fah-vohr.)

2. Where are you from? =
   ¿De dónde es usted?
   (Deh DOHN-deh Ehs Oos-tehd?)

3. I am from the U.S.A. =
   Soy de los Estados Unidos de América. (EE.UU.)
   (Soy Deh Lohs Ehs-tah-dohs Oo-knee-dohs Deh Ah-MEH-ree-kah.)

LESSON 2: CONNECT AND CHAT

27 = VEINTISIETE

A common question is, "Which language is easier to learn, Spanish or English?" The answer is both languages have challenging aspects, but anything can be learned if you are willing to put in the effort. English is a combination of Latin and Germanic rules. Since Spanish is based on Latin rules, there are similarities between English and Spanish.

PHRASES TO CONNECT IN SPANISH

Practice these five phrases that help to communicate in Spanish and connect with others. Read the phrase out loud using the italics to help you with your pronunciation. Note: The number chart from #24 = veinticuatro will help you with more numbers 1-9,000.

1. What is your phone number? =
   ¿Cuál es su número de teléfono?
   (Coo/AHL Ehs Soo NOO-meh-roh Deh Teh-LEH-foh-noh?)

2. My phone number is (967) 555-1384. =
   Mi número de teléfono es (967) 555-1384.
   (Mee NOO-meh-roh Deh Teh-LEH-foh-noh Ehs Noo/eh-veh, Seh/ace, See/eh-teh, Seen-koh, Seen-koh, Seen-koh, Treh-seh Oh-chen-tah Ee Coo/ah-troh.)

3. What is your address? =
   ¿Cuál es su dirección?
   (Coo/AHL Ehs Soo Dee-rehk-see/OHN?)

4. My address is 246 Main Street. =
   Mi dirección es Calle Principal 246.
   (Mee Dee-rehk-see/OHN Ehs Kah-yeh Preen-see-pahl Doh-see/ehn-tohs Coo/ah-rent-tah Ee Seh/ace.)

5. How do you say ___ in Spanish? =
   ¿Cómo se dice ___ en español?
   (KOH-moh Seh Dee-seh ___ Ehn Ehs-pah-ñyohl?)

LESSON 2: CONNECT AND CHAT

28 = VEINTIOCHO

Circle the English choice that matches the Spanish phrase.

1. ¿Cuál es su dirección?
   a. What is your phone number?
   b. Can I have directions?
   c. What is your address?
   d. Which direction is the museum?

2. ¿De dónde es usted?
   a. Where is the bathroom?
   b. Where did you go?
   c. Where are you from?
   d. Where is it located?

3. Mi dirección es Calle Principal 246.
   a. Give the principal the directions.
   b. Direct me to Main Street 246.
   c. 2468-Give me directions, it's late.
   d. My address is 246 Main Street.

4. ¿Cuál es su número de teléfono?
   a. What is your phone number?
   b. What is your favorite number?
   c. Do you have a telephone?
   d. Could I borrow your phone?

29 = VEINTINUEVE

Have you heard some of the numbers in Spanish from Dora or Sesame Street? Knowing the numbers in Spanish is important for traveling in Latin America and communicating with Hispanics. In Spanish, periods and commas are reversed from English. For example, periods are used in the thousands, instead of a comma. In Latin America. 3,000 would be written as 3.000. Commas are used in prices when we use periods. For example, in the U.S.A. we write: $5.84, versus $5,84 in Latin America. The exception is the countries that use the U.S. dollar as their currency. In Mexico, you may see a peso written with one line ($) and a dollar sign with two lines ($) to distinguish the difference.

Say los números = the numbers from 1- 9,000 out loud using the number chart from #24 = veinticuatro. Starting with the second row, notice any patterns and similarities as you read across the rows. If these grammar concepts are too confusing, concentrate on the flashcards and phrases from these lessons and just keep practicing. Keep the flashcards in a small plastic bag, envelope, or in your wallet and practice as much as possible during the week. Place one phrase a day on your refrigerator, mirror, or computer and learn a few at a time. Another idea is to separate all of the flashcards with questions. Use these question cards to interview Hispanic employees or Spanish-speaking friends during the week. Conversing with fluent Spanish speakers is the best way to build up your skills.

LESSON 2: CONNECT AND CHAT

30 = TREINTA

Play a game called, "More or Less = Más o Menos." When having a tough day, Hispanics will answer the question, "¿Cómo está? = How are you?" with the reply, "más o menos." For our "más o menos" game you will need partners. One partner will think of a number between 1 and 1,000. The other person will then try to guess the number in Spanish. If the guessed number is too low, the partner will say, "más." If the guessed number is too high, the partner will say, "menos." Of course, all numbers guessed must be done in Spanish. For example, 492 = cuatrocientos noventa y dos. Numbers and price negotiation are important when you are shopping in Latin America. Use the chart from #24 = veinticuatro to help you.

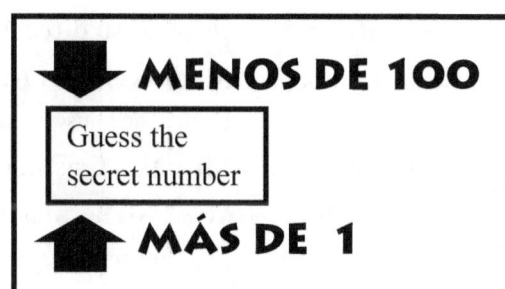

31 = TREINTA Y UNO

Practice these four phrases that you may use when shopping. Negotiating and haggling prices is very common in Latin America.

1. How much does it cost? =
   ¿Cuánto cuesta?
   (Coo/AHN-toh Coo/ehs-tah?)

2. It costs $15. =
   Cuesta 15 dólares.
   (Coo/ehs-tah Keen-seh DOH-Lah-rehs.)

3. Sign here. =
   Firme aquí.
   (Feer-meh Ah-KEE.)

4. You're welcome. Have a great day. =
   De nada. Que tenga un buen día.
   (Deh Nah-dah.) (Keh Tehn-gah Oon Bwhen DEE-ah.)

LESSON 2: CONNECT AND CHAT

32 = TREINTA Y DOS

Now that you have seen all of the 12 phrases, it is time to put them together for a conversation. Have one person say the lines for Diego Rivera and the other person say the lines for Frida Kahlo. Then switch roles. If you have a group, have two people present this as a skit.

Diego Rivera: Hola, Cristina.
Frida Kahlo: Me llamo Frida. Cristina es mi hermana.
Diego Rivera: ¿Cuál es su dirección?
Frida Kahlo: Mi dirección es Avenida Central 1534.
(Note: The house number usually follows the street name in Latin America)
Diego Rivera: Mi amiga Cristina Kahlo vive en Avenida Central 1534.
Frida Kahlo: Yo sé. Mi hermana Cristina vive conmigo.
(I know. = Yo sé.) (with me = conmigo)
Diego Rivera: ¿Cuál es su número de teléfono?
Frida Kahlo: 3-33-12-34
Diego Rivera: Mi amiga Cristina tiene este número.
Frida Kahlo: Yo sé. ¡Nosotros vivimos en la misma casa! (same = misma)

THE AZTEC CALENDAR / SUN STONE = PIEDRA DEL SOL, IS ON DISPLAY IN MEXICO CITY.

LESSON 2: CONNECT AND CHAT

33 = TREINTA Y TRES

Before doing this role play, fill in the blanks for Estudiante #2 with your own real information or use fake data.

Estudiante #1	Buenas tardes. ¿Cuál es su número de teléfono?
Estudiante #2	(_____) _____.
Estudiante #1	¿Cuáles son los últimos 4 números de su seguro social?
Estudiante #2	7689 (= last 4 digits of your Social Security number)
Estudiante #1	¿Cuál es su apellido?
Estudiante #2	Mi apellido es _____. (last name = apellido)
Estudiante #1	¿Cuál es su dirección?
Estudiante #2	Mi dirección es _____.
Estudiante #1	¿Dónde vive usted?
Estudiante #2	Vivo en la ciudad de _____. (city = ciudad)
Estudiante #1	¿Cuál es el estado donde vive?
Estudiante #2	Vivo en el estado de _____. (state = estado)
Estudiante #1	¿Cuál es su código postal? (ZIP code = código postal)
Estudiante #2	Mi código postal es _____.
Estudiante #1	Gracias. Hasta luego.
Estudiante #2	De nada. Hasta luego.

Now find a partner. Have one person play the role of Estudiante #1. This person (Estudiante #1) will ask questions and write down Estudiante #2's Spanish answers in the following blanks. Estudiante #1 has to write down the Spanish numbers and information they hear without peeking at Estudiante #2's paper. After finishing, Estudiante #2 will look at what is written to check if the Spanish answers are correct. Finally, switch roles.

Partner's phone number _____

Last 4 digits of SSN _____

Last name _____

Address _____

City _____

State _____

Zip code _____

LESSON 2: CONNECT AND CHAT

34 = TREINTA Y CUATRO

You probably have a few preguntas = questions. Read these question words and make a list of five questions you would like to ask Hispanic friends or Spanish-speakers that you meet. Choose from these questions or form your own questions relating to your interests. Share two questions with the group.

WHO? = ¿QUIÉN?
Who is it? = ¿Quién es?

THERE ARE THREE WAYS OF SAYING WHAT:

#1 WHAT? = ¿CUÁL? *Use when selecting a choice from a group or with numbers. Which?*
What is your phone number? = ¿Cuál es su número de teléfono?
What is your address? = ¿Cuál es su dirección?

#2 WHAT? = ¿QUÉ? *Use when the answer is a specific item and for telling time.*
What time is it? = ¿Qué hora es?
What is this? = ¿Qué es esto?

#3 WHAT? = ¿CÓMO? = *What did you just say? How's that?*
What is your name? (How are you called?) = ¿Cómo se llama usted?
How are you? = ¿Cómo está usted?
How do you say _____ in Spanish? = ¿Cómo se dice _____ en español?

WHERE? = ¿DÓNDE? Where are you from? = ¿De dónde es usted?
I'm from _____. = Soy de _____. (Place of birth)

WHEN? = ¿CUÁNDO? When is the meeting? = ¿Cuándo es la reunión?
When is your birthday? = ¿Cuándo es su cumpleaños?

WHY? = ¿POR QUÉ?
Why do you study Spanish? = ¿Por qué estudia usted español?

BECAUSE = PORQUE
I study Spanish because I want to talk with my work colleagues. =
Estudio español porque quiero hablar con mis compañeros de trabajo.

HOW MUCH/MANY? = ¿CUÁNTO/CUÁNTA?
How much time until it is finished? = ¿Cuánto tiempo más para terminarlo?
How old is _____? = ¿Cuántos años tiene _____?

35 = TREINTA Y CINCO

In each lesson there will be general information on the various Spanish-speaking countries and cultural considerations. It's important to realize not all Spanish-speakers come from México. All of these Hispanic countries have unique histories, traditions and cultures. These sections will highlight a few of the famous folks and traditional foods, although there are many more that can be found on the Internet. The sample information provided will serve as a way of comparing and contrasting the countries. Here is a brief description of what this information means in each lesson:

- La Moneda Nacional signifies the name of the currency. You will notice some of the countries use the U.S. dollar.

- Los Lugares Para Visitar means the places to visit. This will include some of the major cities and famous attractions associated with the country.

- La Población signifies population. For example the U.S. Population is estimated at around 322 million.

- La Gente Famosa = the famous people

- La Comida = the food

- El Ingreso Anual = the annual income per capita in terms of U.S. dollars also known as the Gross National Income (GNI). Some people are surprised when they compare what the average worker in the United States makes with the salary of workers in other countries. For example the average worker in the United States makes roughly $55,000 while workers in some Latin American countries make less than $2,000 a year! The World Bank is the source for this information throughout this book. Population estimates are from the United Nations.

LESSON 2: CONNECT AND CHAT

36 = TREINTA Y SEIS

EL PAÍS	SPAIN = ESPAÑA	MEXICO = MÉXICO—ESTADOS UNIDOS MEXICANOS
LA MONEDA NACIONAL	Euro	Mexican Peso
LOS LUGARES PARA VISITAR	**Madrid** • *La Capital* • *Museo Nacional del Prado* • *Palacio Real* • *Puerta del Sol* **Granada** • *Alhambra* **San Sebastián** • *Basque region* • *La playa = the beach* **Sevilla** • *Cathedral* • *Alcázar is a royal palace/fort* **Barcelona** • *Las Ramblas street* • *La Sagrada Familia church* • *Plaza de Colón* • *Barrio Gótico* **Toledo** • *Cathedral*	**México City D.F. / Distrito Federal** • *La Capital* • *Zócalo* • *Catedral Nacional* • *Ruinas del Templo Mayor* • *Museo Nacional de Antropología* • *Palacio de Bellas Artes* **Teotihuacan** **Acapulco/Cancún** • *La Playa and Isla Mujeres* • *Chichén Itza Mayan ruins* **Oaxaca** • *Chocolate* • *Mole Sauce on Chicken* • *Monte Albán and Mitla Zapotec ruins* **Guanajuato** • *Silver* • *Museo Casa Diego Rivera* • *Mummies* **Barrancas del Cobre = Copper Canyon**
LA POBLACIÓN	47 million	122 million
LA GENTE FAMOSA	**Rey Juan Carlos I & Reina Sofía (Both born in 1938)** • *King/Queen (1975-2014)* **Isabel de Castilla (1451–1504) & Ferdinand II de Aragón (1452–1516)** • *King/Queen* **Hernán Cortés (1485–1547)** • *Conquistador del México* **Francisco Pizarro (1474-1541)** • *Conquistador del Perú* **Francisco de Goya (1746–1828)** • *Painters* **Pablo Picasso (1881–1973)** • *Painter* **Antoni Gaudí (1852–1926)** • *Architect* **Penélope Cruz Sánchez (Born 1974)** • *Actress* **Antonio Banderas (Born 1960)** • *Actor*	**Diego Rivera (1886–1957)** • *Artist* **Frida Kahlo (1907–1954)** • *Artist* **Octavio Paz (1914–1998)** • *Nobel Prize for Literature 1990* **Sor Juana Inés de la Cruz (1651-1695)** • *Famous writer* **Francisco "Pancho" Villa (1878–1923)** • *Revolutionary* **Emiliano Zapata (1879–1919)** • *Leader of peasant rebellion* **Moctezuma (1466-1520)** • *Aztec Ruler* **La Malinche/Doña Mariana (1505-1529)** • *Translator for Cortés*
EL INGRESO ANUAL = ANNUAL INCOME (GNI)	$32,030 per year	$16,110 per year

EL PAÍS	SPAIN = ESPAÑA		MEXICO = MÉXICO—ESTADOS UNIDOS MEXICANOS	
LA COMIDA	**Paella** • Yellow saffron rice **Tortilla Española** • An egg and potato omelet **Tapas** • Appetizers, the name tapa comes from "tapar" to cover.	**Jamón Serrano** • Thinly sliced cured ham **Vino** • Wine from La Rioja **Aceite de Oliva** • Olive oil Spain produces 36% of world supply **Turrón** • Almond marzipan bark	**Tortillas** • Flat, round, unleavened bread made of corn **Tacos/ Burritos Con Frijoles** **Mole Poblano** • A brown sauce made with ground seeds or nuts, Mexican chocolate, dried chilies, garlic, onions, and spices	**Enchiladas** • Tortillas rolled with meat inside baked in sauce **Chapulines** • Roasted crickets **Salsas/Guacamole** • Avocado smashed with chile and spices **Tequila** • Alcoholic drink made from the Maguey (Agave) plant

37 = TREINTA Y SIETE

Read these three trivia statements about Spain and Mexico. Two sentences are true and one is false. Guess which one is not true. The previous cultural section does not contain the answers, so check the Answer Key to find out why one of them is not culturally correct.

INTERESTING THINGS = COSAS INTERESANTES:

1. _____ Frida Kahlo was married to Diego Rivera and they lived in La Casa Azul = The Blue House in México City.

2. _____ The Aztecs had a dream that they should build México City on the spot where they found an eagle holding a cactus in its mouth.

3. _____ Construction on La Sagrada Familia Church in Barcelona began in 1882 and may finish around 2026. The word gaudy comes from the ornate, garish style of the church's designer, Antoni Gaudí.

FOOD = COMIDA:

1. _____ If you order a "Tortilla con queso" in Spain you would get something like a Quesadilla with a flour taco shell.

2. _____ Mole sauce can be verde (green), amarillo (yellow), negro (black), or coloradito/rojo (red) and is served over chicken.

3. _____ Calamares en su tinta = Squid in its own ink can turn your mouth black as you eat it.

LESSON 2: CONNECT AND CHAT

38 = TREINTA Y OCHO

One of the great joys of studying Spanish is the discovery of the great diversity of the language and the unique slang in each country. Just as in English there are different ways of saying the same thing.

- For example, carro is car in México; coche is car in Spain, but pig in Guatemala. A tortilla, which is a flour shell in México, is a potato omelet in Spain. Taco is a food in México. A taco is the heel of a shoe in Argentina and tacones are high heals. A taco in Chile is a traffic jam. In Costa Rica parents tell their children not to say "tacos" which means "bad words." This book does not contain any "tacos," so you will have to learn those on your own, we will concentrate on "clean" conversations.

- Native speakers often identify a person's origin by listening to their accent or slang. We have the same concept in English. The English spoken in the United States, Australia and the United Kingdom is slightly different but is still considered English. The same is true in the Spanish-speaking countries. Castilian Spanish from Spain tends to be the most formal and proper. When you listen to a native speaker from Spain, they may use the "th" sound for "S" for example, "gracias" would sound like *(Grah-thee/ahs)*.

- In places bordering México, "Spanglish" words combining English and Spanish are used more frequently especially in households and family environments. As you listen to Spanish, try to guess where the person is from.

- The best way to learn Spanish is to memorize one way of saying a phrase and then add more ideas/concepts as your skill level advances. The phrases in this book will generally be understood in all of the Spanish-speaking countries.

- A common question is, "Why shouldn't everyone learn English?" The answer is many people are trying to learn English. After these Spanish lessons, you realize learning another language is not that easy.

- English language fluency increases according to how many generations of the family have resided in the United States. For example, the Pew Hispanic Center reported only 23% of first-generation Hispanics spoke English very well. This increased to 88% by the second generation and 94% of third or higher generations. In fact, many third-generation Hispanic/Chicanos may not even speak Spanish. Did this happen with a language in your family history?

39 = TREINTA Y NUEVE

Write the letter of the corresponding English phrase on the line next to the Spanish phrase.

1. _____ Mi dirección es Calle Principal 246.

2. _____ ¿Cuál es su dirección?

3. _____ ¿De dónde es usted?

4. _____ ¿Cuál es su número de teléfono?

5. _____ Cuesta 15 dólares.

6. _____ Espere un momento, por favor.

7. _____ Que tenga un buen día.

8. _____ ¿Cómo se dice ___ en español?

9. _____ De nada.

10. _____ ¿Cuánto cuesta?

11. _____ Soy de los Estados Unidos de América.

12. _____ Mi número de teléfono es (967) 555-1384.

13. _____ Firme aquí.

A. *(ah)* Sign here.

B. *(beh)* You're welcome.

C. *(seh)* My phone number is (967) 555-1384.

D. *(deh)* Please wait one moment.

E. *(eh)* My address is 246 Main Street.

F. *(ehf-feh)* It costs $15.

G. *(heh)* What is your address?

H. *(ah-cheh)* How much does it cost?

I. *(eeee)* How do you say ___ in Spanish?

J. *(hoh-tah)* I am from the U.S.A.

K. *(kah)* What is your phone number?

L. *(ehl-leh)* Have a great day.

M. *(ehm-meh)* Where are you from?

# 40 = CUARENTA

Play the game of "Toma Todo." Cut the flashcards on the following page apart, or make your own. Each player chooses 10 flashcards he or she would like to practice from Lessons 1 and 2. The first person to run out of flashcards loses the game. Note: If you roll a Toma and there are no flashcards in the middle then your turn is over and the next person rolls. Also, when one person says them in Spanish, the other player could try to say them in English without peeking at the back of the flashcard. This game can be played in partners, a group of three or by dividing the class into two teams.

IF YOU ROLL A 1 - TOMA 1 = TAKE 1
You take one from the center and say it in Spanish.

IF YOU ROLL A 2 - TOMA 2 = TAKE 2
You take two from the center and say them in Spanish.

IF YOU ROLL A 3 - PON 1 = PUT 1
You put one in the center and say it in Spanish.

IF YOU ROLL A 4 - PON 2 = PUT 2
You put two in the center and say them in Spanish.

IF YOU ROLL A 5 - TODOS PONEN = EVERYONE PUTS ONE.
Each player has to put one in the center and say it in Spanish

IF YOU ROLL A 6 - *TOMA TODO* = TAKE EVERYTHING.
¡Jackpot! Take all the pieces from the center and as an extra bonus you don't have to say anything.

LESSON 2: CONNECT AND CHAT

Please wait one moment. *LESSON 2*	Sign here. *LESSON 2*	You're welcome. Have a great day. *LESSON 2*
How do you say ___ in Spanish? *LESSON 2*	Where are you from? *LESSON 2*	What is your phone number? *LESSON 2*
My phone number is (967) 555-1384. *LESSON 2*	What is your address? *LESSON 2*	My address is 246 Main Street. *LESSON 2*
How much does it cost? *LESSON 2*	It costs $15. *LESSON 2*	I am from the U.S.A. *LESSON 2*

LESSON 2: CONNECT AND CHAT

De nada. *(Deh Nah-dah.)* Que tenga un buen día. *(Keh Tehn-gah Oon Bwhen DEE-ah.)*	Firme aquí. *(Feer-meh Ah-KEE.)*	Espere un momento, por favor. *(Ehs-peh-reh Oon Moh-mehn-toh, Pohr Fah-vohr.)*
¿Cuál es su número de teléfono? *(Coo/AHL Ehs Soo NOO-meh-roh Deh Teh-LEH-foh-noh?)*	¿De dónde es usted? *(Deh DOHN-deh Ehs Oos-tehd?)*	¿Cómo se dice ___ en español? *(KOH-moh Seh Dee-seh ___ Ehn Ehs-pah-ñyohl?)*
Mi dirección es Calle Principal 246. *(Mee Dee-rehk-see/OHN Ehs Kah-yeh Preen-see-pahl Doh-see/ehn-tohs Coo/ah-rent-tah Ee Seh/ace.)*	¿Cuál es su dirección? *(Coo/AHL Ehs Soo Dee-rehk-see/OHN?)*	Mi número de teléfono es (967) 555-1384. *(Mee NOO-meh-roh Deh Teh-LEH-foh-noh Ehs Noo/eh-veh, Seh/ace, See/eh-teh, Seen-koh, Seen-koh, Seen-koh, Treh-seh Oh-chen-tah Ee Coo/ah-troh.)*
Soy de los Estados Unidos de América. *(Soy Deh Lohs Ehs-tah-dohs Oo-knee-dohs Deh Ah-MEH-ree-kah.)*	Cuesta 15 dólares. *(Coo/ehs-tah Keen-seh DOH-Lah-rehs.)*	¿Cuánto cuesta? *(Coo/AHN-toh Coo/ehs-tah?)*

41 = CUARENTA Y UNO

Spanish is often referred to as a "Romance Language." All Latin-based languages like Italian, French and Portuguese are considered "Romance Languages." One reason for this is because all nouns have either a masculine or feminine gender, even the table = la mesa.

THE FOUR WAYS OF SAYING "THE," INVENTED JUST TO CONFUSE US

In Spanish the "el" before the noun makes the word masculine. For example, el libro means the book. In Spanish the "la" before the word makes the word feminine. For example, la casa means the house. If the noun is plural, then the article changes to "los" if it is masculine or "las" if it is feminine. For example, los libros means the books and las casas means the houses.

	SINGULAR	PLURAL
MALE	**el** el niño = the male child	**los** los niños = the children (at least 1 male)
FEMALE	**la** la niña = the female child	**las** las niñas = the children (all females)

HOW DO YOU KNOW WHICH ONE TO USE?

Normally if a noun ends in the letter o it's masculine, and if it ends in the letter a it's feminine. However, that is not always the case. For example, el día, el problema and la mano are just a few examples where there are exceptions to the rule.

- Masculine nouns frequently end in –o –os –l –ma

- Feminine nouns frequently end with –a –as –dad –tad –tud –ción –sión

- Nouns ending in –ista and –e, can use either el, la, los, or las depending on gender.

Now practice what you've learned. Fill in the blanks with either el, la, los, or las.

1. _____ hermana   2. _____ hermanos   3. _____ cuenta   4. _____ plato

5. _____ tenedores   6. _____ cuchillo   7. _____ cuchara   8. _____ tazas

LESSON 2: CONNECT AND CHAT

42 = CUARENTA Y DOS

Complete the crossword puzzle by using words from each of the eight Spanish phrases from 26 = veintisés and 27 = veintisiete Find the opposite translation. If the clue is in Spanish, then write the English phrase. If the clue is in English, then write the Spanish phrase. There are no punctuation marks or spaces between words. Check your answers in the Answer Key when you are finished. Good luck! = ¡Buena suerte!

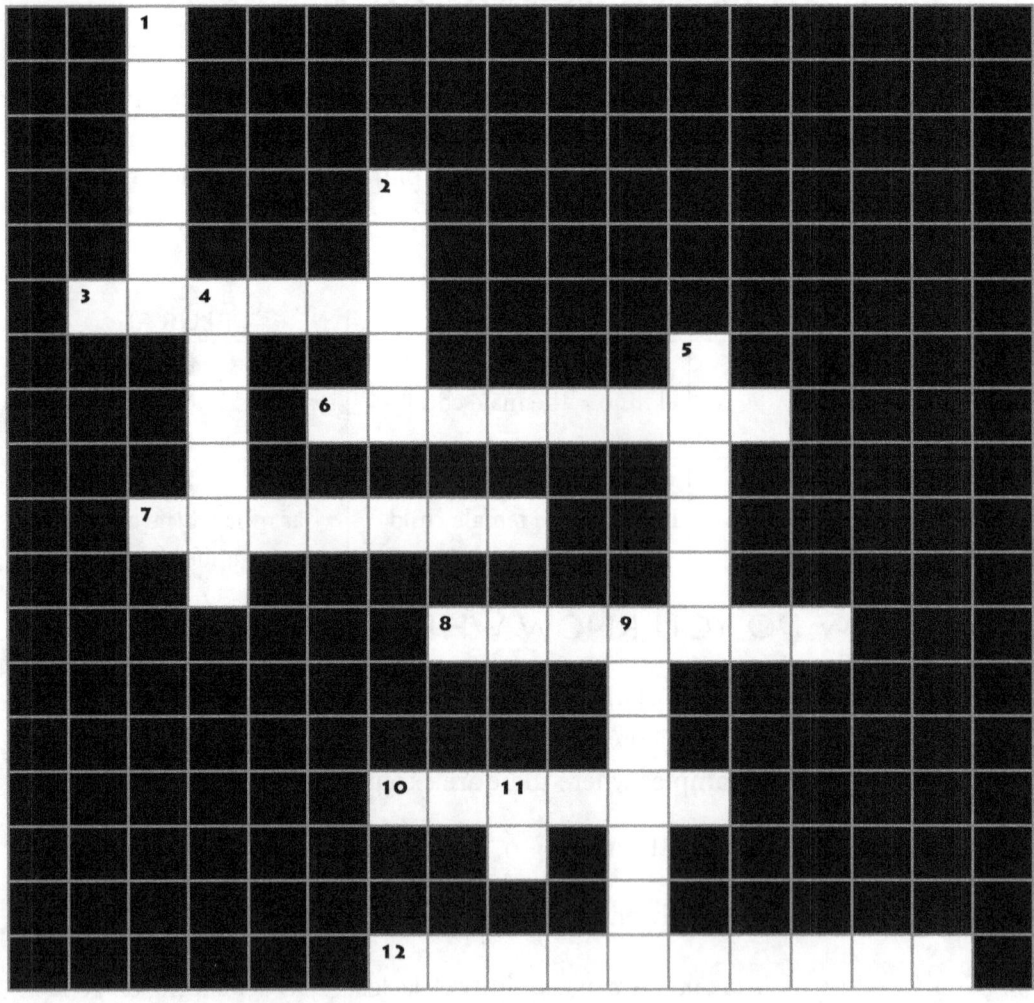

HORIZONTAL
3. WAIT
6. TELEPHONE
7. SPANISH
8. STATES
10. NUMBER
12. HOW DO YOU SAY

VERTICAL
1. CUÁL ES
2. DÓNDE
4. POR FAVOR
5. UNIDOS
9. DIRECCIÓN
11. MI

SPANISH CHATBOOK ❶ © SPANISH CHAT COMPANY

43 = CUARENTA Y TRES

Translate these phrases. Write the English for the first six phrases and write the Spanish for the last six phrases. This may be done as an exam or as homework for the next lesson. When finished check your answers in the Answer Key. Note that "translate" is written translation and "interpret" is orally communicating. That is the difference between a translator and an interpretor.

1. Cuesta 15 dólares. _____

2. ¿Cuál es su número de teléfono? _____

3. De nada. Que tenga un buen día. _____

4. Firme aquí. _____

5. ¿Cómo se dice ___ en español? _____

6. ¿De dónde es usted? _____

7. I am from the U.S.A.. _____

8. What is your address? _____

9. How much does it cost? _____

10. My phone number is (967) 555-1384. _____

11. Please wait one moment. _____

12. My address is 246 Main Street. _____

LESSON 2: CONNECT AND CHAT

UN ANUNCIO = AN AD

DO YOU NEED ANYTHING ELSE? = ¿NECESITA ALGO MÁS?

Want to order more books for coworkers, friends, or your entire company?
Here is how: Order online at SpanishChatCompany.com

ONLINE GAMES, FLASHCARDS, ACTIVITIES & VIDEOS

SpanishChatCompany.com

MINI-CHATBOOKS

CHAT ABOUT THE FAMILY

GOALS: In this lesson you will learn about these topics: the Mayan number system, personal questions to establish rapport, gender differences, machismo, Hispanic families, locating Central American countries, expressing likes and dislikes, describing your family, your job, your age, Central American countries; Guatemala, El Salvador, Honduras, Nicaragua, Costa Rica and Panama, family ties, alphabet, travel advice, spelling and best wishes.

LESSON 3: CHAT ABOUT THE FAMILY

44 = CUARENTA Y CUATRO

Read these phrases and answers from Lessons 1 and 2. Change them to fit your own personal information.

1. ¿Cómo está usted? Estoy ocupada y cansada. = I am busy and tired. (female) Estoy_____
_____

2. ¿Cómo se llama usted? Me llamo _____
_____

3. ¿Cuál es su apellido? Mi apellido es Pospishil. _____
_____

4. ¿De dónde es usted? Soy de los EE.UU. de América. _____
_____

5. ¿Cuánto cuesta? Cuesta $100. Es demasiado caro. = It is too expensive. ___
_____

45 = CUARENTA Y CINCO

Guess the English translation of these family members to fill in the blanks. For more family words consult a dictionary.

1. mamá/madre= _____
2. papá/padre =_____
3. hijo = _____
   (mi-jo is slang for mi hijo and means sweetie/darling)
4. hija =_____
   (mi-ja is slang for mi hija and means sweetie/darling)
5. esposo = _____
6. esposa = _____ (The plural "esposas" means handcuffs)

46 = CUARENTA Y SEIS

The accents and gender of a word do make a difference in Spanish. For example, el papá means dad. However, la papa means potato and el Papa means the pope. A crowd may chant, "¡Viva El Papa!" This means long live the Pope. If they chanted, "¡Viva la papa!" this would mean long live the potato. The expression "ni papa" means you don't know any Spanish—not even the word potato. Luckily you will now know papa is potato in Latin America and patata is potato in Spain. If someone asks if you speak Spanish, answer with "ni papa" and you might get a big smile.

47 = CUARENTA Y SIETE

One of the great Pre-Columbian civilizations was the Maya Empire. Math is one area in which they made many contributions. The Maya were the first people to use the concept of zero. Zero was depicted in the Mayan writing system with a drawing of a seashell. The Mayan numbers 1–19 which were originally formed by using sticks and stones:

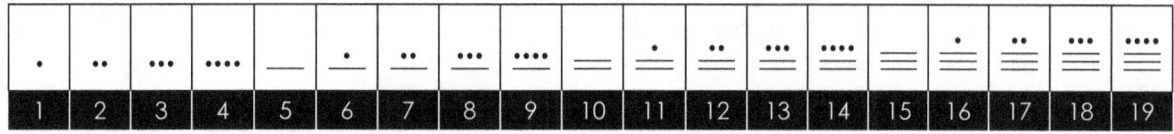

Now invent four of your own math problems using the Mayan numbers.

For example, _____ + ••• = •••

1. _____

2. _____

3. _____

4. _____

LESSON 3: CHAT ABOUT THE FAMILY

48 = CUARENTA Y OCHO

These six phases will help you ask personal questions to build rapport. When you begin to try out your Spanish skills, sometimes you will get yourself into confusing situations. When speaking with a Spanish-speaking friend use what you already know and try out your detective skills to guess the rest. Relax and have fun because many Hispanics are honored that you are trying to learn their language and relieved that they aren't relying on their own English skills.

1. Where do you work? =
   ¿Dónde trabaja?
   (DOHN-deh Trah-bah-hah?)

2. I work in a school. =
   Trabajo en una escuela.
   (Trah-bah-hoh Ehn Oo-nah Ehs-kweh-lah.)

3. What is your daughter's name? =
   ¿Cómo se llama su hija?
   (KOH-moh Seh Yah-mah Soo Ee-hah?)

4. My daughter's name is Rose. =
   Mi hija se llama Rosa.
   (Mee Ee-hah Seh Yah-mah Roh-sah.)

5. How old are your children? =
   ¿Cuántos años tienen sus hijos?
   (Coo/AHN-tohs Ah-ñyohs Tee-eh-nehn Soos Ee-hohs?)

6. My children are 11 and 13 years old. =
   Mis hijos tienen once y trece años.
   (Mees Ee-hohs Tee-eh-nehn Ohn-seh Ee Treh-seh Ah-ñyohs.)

49 = CUARENTA Y NUEVE

Read this chart and then circle the answer to each of the four questions below in your own opinion, using either me gusta or no me gusta. For more practice try our Spanish Chatbook 2.

I like the chocolate. = Me gusta el chocolate.	I don't like the chocolate. = No me gusta el chocolate.
I like the chocolates. (more than one chocolate) = Me gustan los chocolates.	I don't like the chocolates. (more than one chocolate) = No me gustan los chocolates.
He/She/You (formal) likes the chocolate. = Le gusta el chocolate.	Do you like chocolate? = ¿Le gusta el chocolate?

1. ¿Le gusta la comida aquí? = the food here

    Me gusta la comida aquí. / No me gusta la comida aquí.

2. ¿Le gusta el café con leche? = coffee with milk

    Me gusta el café con leche. / No me gusta el café con leche.

3. ¿Le gusta su trabajo? = job

    Me gusta mi trabajo. / No me gusta mi trabajo.

4. ¿Le gustan los libros? = books (use gustan)

    Me gustan los libros. / No me gustan los libros.

Next, ask a partner the same four questions and write their answer below They will answer in Spanish with either Me gusta = I like or No me gusta = I don't like.

1. ¿Le gusta la comida aquí? _____

2. ¿Le gusta el café con leche? _____

3. ¿Le gusta su trabajo? _____

4. ¿Le gustan los libros? _____

A GAME = UN JUEGO

Play a game to practice with your group. The first person says, "Me gusta o Me gustan _____." The next person will add on by saying, "Me gusta _____. y a (Julia) le gusta _____." Continue to add on for the rest of the group. Lo siento = Sorry for the last person that has to repeat them for everybody.

LESSON 3: CHAT ABOUT THE FAMILY

50 = CINCUENTA

Read these phrases out loud using the pronunciation column on the right. Leave this chart blank, the next page #51 = cincuenta y uno will have spaces for you to fill in your own information.

ENGLISH:	SPANISH:	PRONUNCIATION GUIDE:
My name is _____.	Me llamo _____.	*Meh Yah-moh* _____.
His/Her name is _____.	Se llama _____.	*Seh Yah-mah* _____.
I live in Omaha.	Yo vivo en Omaha.	*Yo Vee-voh Ehn Oh-mah-hah.*
She lives in _____. He lives in _____.	Ella vive en _____. Él vive en _____.	*Eh-yah Vee-veh Ehn* _____. *EHL Vee-veh Ehn* _____.
I work in _____.	Yo trabajo en _____.	*Yo Trah-bah-hoh Ehn* _____.
She works in _____.	Ella trabaja en _____.	*Eh-Yah Trah-bah-hah Ehn* _____.
He is retired. He/She doesn't work, but goes to school.	Él está jubilado. No trabaja, pero va a la escuela.	*EHL Ehs-TAH Who-bee-lah-doh. No Trah-bah-hah Pehr-oh Vah Ah Lah Ehs-kweh-lah*
I am _____ years old.	Yo tengo _____ años.	*Yo Tehn-goh* _____ *Ah-ñyohs.*
She is _____ years old. He is _____ years old.	Ella tiene _____ años. Él tiene _____ años.	*Eh-yah Tee/eh-neh* _____ *Ah-ñyohs EHL Tee/eh-neh* _____ *Ah-ñyohs.*
I like _____.	Me gusta _____.	*Meh Goose-tah* _____.
He/She likes _____.	Le gusta _____.	*Leh- Goose-tah* _____.

SPANISH CHATBOOK ❶ © SPANISH CHAT COMPANY

LESSON 3: CHAT ABOUT THE FAMILY

51 = CINCUENTA Y UNO

THE FAMILY PROJECT = EL PROYECTO DE LA FAMILIA:

Create your own family project. To begin, read these two sample descriptions. If you have a group, have each person read one sentence out loud.

- 🌎 Me llamo Julia. Yo vivo en Omaha. Yo trabajo en la universidad y en mi casa. Yo tengo 38 años. Tengo dos hijos. Me gusta viajar y hablar por teléfono.

- 🌎 Mi perrita se llama Maya. Ella vive en mi casa. Ella no trabaja. Ella tiene 3 años. No le gustan los gatos.

Now, fill in these blanks for yourself and one of your family members or friends, You will need an extra piece of paper and you can use the chart from # 50 = cincuenta to help you. For the next meeting, you will tell the group in Spanish about your "family." Bring in family pictures or create a computer presentation. If you would rather tell about a famous family like the the Brady Bunch, bring in a picture of them instead. Practice by sharing this with your own family. Note: If you don't want to divulge your age, you can say "-ticinco" = "and five" *(Tee Seen-koh)* like they do in Costa Rica. It could mean 25 (Vein*ticinco*), 35 or 45...

Me llamo _____ . Yo vivo en _____ .
                            name   city

Yo trabajo en _____ .
                      workplace

Yo tengo _____ años. Me gusta _____ .
                       #   something you like

~~~~~~

Mi _____ se llama _____ . Vive en _____ .
    family member/friend   name   city

Trabaja en _____ .
                 workplace

Tiene _____ años. Le gusta _____
              #   something he/she likes

LESSON 3: CHAT ABOUT THE FAMILY

52 = CINCUENTA Y DOS

In many Hispanic countries, family is very important. Asking and taking interest in the Hispanic family is a great way to build rapport. Latin America is still a machismo society, meaning males have a lot of influence in the family. This, however, is slowly changing in the younger generations. It is still very common to work together toward the good of the entire extended family and not emphasize individual goals. Latinos are usually great team members and may even overly agree with their supervisor and authority figures.

Families in Central America = América Central tend to rely on each other even if they move far away from their country. You may see flags, photos, medallions and T-shirts that have been sent from the country of origin as a reminder. In the reverse direction paychecks are wired back to Latin America to help with family expenses.

Some Spanish-speakers enjoy talking about where they are from, and people learning Spanish sometimes don't always remember the names and locations of Mexico and the Spanish-speaking Central American countries on a map. An easy way to know the locations is to remember the phrase, "My grandma happily eats nine chile peppers." In this mnemonic, the first letter of each word represents a Spanish-speaking country below the United States of America starting in México, and continuing from the North down to the South: M = México, G = Guatemala, H = Honduras, E = El Salvador, N = Nicaragua, C = Costa Rica, P = Panamá. The only problem with this system is you have to add "My brave grandma" to add the English-speaking country of Belize, which is east of Guatemala. Belize is the former English colony, British Honduras. Find these countries on the map #12 = doce.

53 = CINCUENTA Y TRES

Six Central American countries speak Spanish, #54 = cincuenta y cuatro has Costa Rica & Panama.

EL PAÍS	GUATEMALA	EL SALVADOR	HONDURAS	NICARAGUA
LA MONEDA NACIONAL	Quetzal	U.S. Dollar/Colón	Lempira	Córdoba
LOS LUGARES PARA VISITAR	**Guatemala City** • La Capital **Antigua** • Colonial City • Volcanoes to climb **Tikal National Park** • Mayan Ruins **Lake Atitlán** • Deepest lake in Central America	**San Salvador** • La Capital **Tazumal** • Mayan Ruins **Los Cobanos** • Fishing **Ilopango market** • Shopping **Ruta de las Flores** **Santa Ana Volcano**	**Tegucigalpa** • La Capital **Copán Ruinas** • Mayan Ruins **Bay Islands** **San Pedro Sula** • History Museum	**Managua** • La Capital **Granada and León** • Colonial Cities **Lake Nicaragua** • Volcanoes - 7 active, 50 total
LA POBLACIÓN	15.5 million	6 million	8.5 million	6 million
LA GENTE FAMOSA	**Rigoberta Menchú Tum (Born 1959)** • Human rights Activist • Nobel Prize Winner 1992 **Ricardo Arjona (Born 1964)** • Singer	**Óscar Romero (1917–1980)** • Archbishop and murdered during Civil War **Christy Turlington (Born 1969)** • Half Salvadoran, Supermodel	**Lempira (1499-1537)** • War captain of the Lencas and fought against the Spanish **Roberto Sosa (1930-2011)** • Poet **Neida Sandoval (Born 1961)** • Television **Satcha Pretto (Born 1980)** • Television	**Rubén Darío (1867–1916)** • Poet **Giocanda Belli (Born 1948)** • Novelist • Poet **Violeta Chamorro (Born 1929)** • First female president in Latin America (1990–1997)
LA COMIDA	**Café** • Coffee **Pepián** • Meat and veggie stew **Licuado** • Fruit juice	**Pupusas** • Thick, corn tortilla **Sopa de Pata** • Soup **Quesadilla** • Sweet cheese pound cake	**Tostones** • Twice fried plantains **Anafres** • Bean/cheese dip served with chips **Yuca Frita** • Fried yucca	**Gallo Pinto** • Red beans and rice **Pan de Coco** • Coconut bread **Mondongo** • Tripe / intestine stew
EL INGRESO ANUAL = ANNUAL INCOME (GNI)	$7,130 per year	$7,490 per year	$4,270 per year	$4,510 per year

54 = CINCUENTA Y CUATRO

Read the information about these final two Central American countries.

EL PAÍS	COSTA RICA	PANAMÁ
LA MONEDA NACIONAL	Colón	U.S. Dollar/Balboa
LOS LUGARES PARA VISITAR	**San José** • *La Capital* • *Teatro Nacional* • *Gold museum)* **Arenal** • *Active Volcano/Hot Springs* **Poás/Iruazú** • *Volcanoes/Craters* **Manuel Antonio National Park** • *Monkeys on the beach* **Monteverde Cloud Forest** **Tamarindo and Playa Langosta** • *Beaches* • *Whales*	**Panama City** • *La Capital* • *Panama canal and the Miraflores locks* • *Casco Antiguo/Viejo is a World Heritage site* **San Blás-Islands** • *Home of the Kunas and molas* **Pearl Islands=Las Perlas** **Bocas del Toro** • *Rainforest and Beach* **Colón** • *Caribbean port* **Boquete** • *Volcán Barú - Chiriquí*
LA POBLACIÓN	5 million	4 million
LA GENTE FAMOSA	**Laura Chinchilla (Born 1959)** • *President 2010-2014* **Óscar Arias (Born 1941)** • *Nobel Peace Prize Winner 1985* • *He helped to end Civil Wars in several Central American countries.* • *President (1986–1990) & (2006–2010)* **Pancha Carrasco (1826–1890)** • *First woman in the military*	**Manuel Noriega (Born 1934)** • *Dictator of Panamá (1983–1989)* • *In 1989 he began serving jail time in Florida for cocaine trafficking, racketeering, and money laundering.* **Rod Carew (Born 1945)** • *In baseball hall of fame* **Rubén Blades (Born 1948)** • *Singer, songwriter, actor* **Gloria Guardia (Born 1940)** • *Novelist, journalist*
LA COMIDA	**Gallo Pinto** • *Black beans and rice usually flavored with cilantro and served with Huevos revueltos = Scrambled eggs* **Flan de Coco** • *Coconut flan* **Café con leche** • *Coffee with milk* **Fresco de frutas** • *Fruit salad*	**Tamales** • *Corn meal dough wrapped in banana leaves* **Patacones de plátano** • *Fried plantains* **Sancocho** • *Stew* **Ceviche** • *Lemon fish* **Empanandas** • *Pastry pockets with filling*
EL INGRESO ANUAL = ANNUAL INCOME (GNI)	$13,570 per year	$14,630 per year

55 = CINCUENTA Y CINCO

Read these three trivia statements about the Central American countries. Two sentences are true and one is false. Guess which one is not true. The previous cultural section does not contain the answers, so check the Answer Key to find out why one of them is not culturally correct.

Note: You may see this sign while you are traveling: El papel higiénico se tira en el cesto de basura, nunca en el inodoro. = Toilet paper is thrown in the trash never in the toilet. Due to plumbing issues, you may have to throw your toilet paper in the trash can in many Central American countries. *Papel* higiénico is used in Latin America as the proper term for toilet paper, but papel del baño is more commonly heard in Mexico. Now you are ready for even more amazing trivia.

INTERESTING THINGS = COSAS INTERESANTES:

1. _____ Tikal, Guatemala was a large, ancient Maya civilization city that included about 3,000 structures.

2. _____ It takes 18 hours and only costs about $18 to go by bus from San José, Costa Rica, to Panamá City, Panamá.

3. _____ Lake Nicaragua is called "Mar Dulce" = Sweet Sea. It is a freshwater lake with no tuna fish or sharks.

FOOD = COMIDA:

1. _____ Anafres bean dip from Honduras is served in a clay pot with hot coals underneath.

2. _____ The Ceviche fish dish is steamed in an oven for about 5 minutes.

3. _____ If you ordered El Salvadorian Sopa de Pata, you may find yucca, plantains, cow's stomach and cow's feet along with some lemon juice and spices in your dish.

LESSON 3: CHAT ABOUT THE FAMILY

56 = CINCUENTA Y SEIS

Practice these three Spanish phrases that will help you discuss your families and family ties. The third line is often used as a sign of courtesy.

TRACK 11

1. How many people are in your family? =
   ¿Cuántas personas hay en su familia?
   (Coo/AHN-tahs Pehr-soh-nahs Eye Ehn Soo Fah-mee-lee/ah?)

2. There are ___ people in my family. =
   Hay ___ personas en mi familia.
   (Eye ___ Pehr-soh-nahs Ehn Mee Fah-mee-lee/ah.)

3. Do you have animals? =
   ¿Tiene animales?
   (Tee/eh-neh Ah-nee-mah-lehs?)

   Note: Do you have pets? = ¿Tiene mascotas?

UN POCO MÁS = A LITTLE MORE

Circle the English choice that matches the Spanish phrase.

1. Hay ___ personas en mi familia.
   a. My ___ have a lot of hay.
   b. My ___ family is over there.
   c. Those ___ people in that family eat hay.
   d. There are ___ people in my family.

2. ¿Tiene un perro o un gato?
   a. Do you have animals?
   b. Do you have a pear or a gate?
   c. Do you have a dog or a cat?
   d. Can I borrow your dog or cat?

3. ¿Cómo se llama su hijo?
   a. What is your son's name?
   b. What is your name?
   c. Where is your son?
   d. Is your son coming to visit?

4. ¿Cuántas personas hay en su familia?
   a. How many parrots are there?
   b. Can your family come over?
   c. How many people are in your family?
   d. How many people are coming?

57 = CINCUENTA Y SIETE

Have one person say the lines for Rigoberta Menchú, a child, and the other person say the lines for Rubén Darío, who is working as a telemarketer. Then switch roles. If you have a group, have two people present this as a skit.

Rubén Darío: Hola. Me llamo Rubén. ¿Cómo se llama?

Rigoberta Menchú: Me llamo Rigoberta.

Rubén Darío: ¿Cuál es su apellido?

Rigoberta Menchú: Mis apellidos son Menchú Tum.
Note: For two last names use, "mis apellidos son..."

Rubén Darío: ¿Cuántas personas hay en su familia?

Rigoberta Menchú: Hay cinco personas en mi familia.

Rubén Darío: ¿Dónde trabaja?

Rigoberta Menchú: No trabajo. Voy a la escuela. =I go to school.

Rubén Darío: Perdón, pero... ¿cuántos años tiene?

Rigoberta Menchú: Yo tengo diez años.

Rubén Darío: Ay, Ay, Ay. ¿Me permite hablar con su mamá?

Rigoberta Menchú: Sí, claro que sí. ¡Mamáááááá!

Work with a partner or individually to write your own conversation or role play that highlights a typical situation or scenarios from your life. Include questions, problems, solutions and/or phrases from Lessons 1–3. Present this new conversation in front of the group.

LESSON 3: CHAT ABOUT THE FAMILY

58 = CINCUENTA Y OCHO

Read or sing the alphabet = el alfabeto out loud using the following pronunciation guide to help you. Note: The letters CH, LL, RR used to be considered as separate letters in the Spanish alphabet, until the Real Academia Española eliminated them in the 1990's.

THE ALPHABET = EL ALFABETO:

A	ah	Ñ	ehn-ñyeh
B	beh	O	oh
C	seh	P	peh
D	deh	Q	koo
E	eh	R	air-reh
F	ehf-feh	S	ehs-seh
G	heh	T	teh
H	ah-cheh	U	oo
I	eee OR (eee Latina) *(Latina literally means the Latin Eee)*	V	veh OR (oo-veh)
J	hoh-tah	W	doh-bleh-veh OR (doh-bleh-oo) *(In Spain = oo-veh doh-bleh)*
K	kah	X	eh-kees
L	ehl-leh	Y	yeh OR (ee-gree-eh-gah) *(Griega literally means the Greek Eee)*
M	ehm-meh	Z	seh-tah
N	ehn-neh		

59 = CINCUENTA Y NUEVE

THE PIÑATA GAME = EL JUEGO DE LA PIÑATA:

Here are two games to practice with the alphabet. With a partner, spell each other's Spanish names or middle names or favorite Spanish word. Ask your partner, "**¿Cómo se escribe eso?** = How do you spell (write) that?" One person spells and the partner writes down the letters, until they guess the word.

Play a game called Piñata. This game is like hangman. Each person thinks of a Spanish phrase from Lessons 1–3 and writes down the exact number of lines to correspond to each letter in the phrase. The difference is you start with a 7-point star piñata and fill in one of each of the triangles for each wrong guess. The first person to fill their piñata loses the game.

Latin Americans have been using candies and small toys to fill up piñatas for many years. Piñatas may have originated in Europe with a painted clay pot filled with candies and coins. A star-shaped piñata probably represented the Star of Bethlehem at Christmas time and is still used in the December Posadas celebrations. Now there are many designs from animals to cartoon characters. Find Web sites showing different styles of piñatas. To make your own piñata, see directions on the internet. In Cuba they attach strings to the piñata and instead of using a bat, everyone grabs a string and pulls the piñata apart.

LESSON 3: CHAT ABOUT THE FAMILY

60 = SESENTA

¡AY AY AY! = Uh oh! Are you having trouble understanding someone's name. Use the first phrase to ask them to spell it. Use the second phrase for birthdays or any great news. Since family is so important to many people, it is considered very polite to use the third phrase.

TRACK 13

1. How do you spell (write) that? =
   ¿Cómo se escribe eso?
   (KOH-moh Seh Ehs-cree-beh Ehs-oh?)

2. Best wishes! =
   ¡Felicidades!
   (Feh-lee-see-dah-dehs!)

3. Greetings to your family. =
   Saludos a su familia.
   (Sah-loo-dohs Ah Soo Fah-mee-lee/ah.)

Practice your pronunciation with these tongue twisters. Listen to the native speakers on the audio version and try repeating them quickly.

TONGUE TWISTERS = TRABALENGUAS:

TRACK 14

1. Pepe puso un peso en el piso del pozo. En el piso del pozo, Pepe puso un peso. = Pepe put a peso at the bottom of the well. At the bottom of the well, Pepe put a peso.

TRACK 15

2. Erre con erre guitarra, erre con erre carril. Rápido corren los carros, cargados de azúcar del ferrocarril. = R with an R, guitar. R with an R, lane. The train cars go quickly, filled with sugar from the railroad.

TRACK 16

3. Compadre, cómpreme un coco. Compadre, coco no compro, porque como poco coco como, poco coco compro.
   Pal, buy me a coconut. Pal, I don't buy coconuts, because I eat very few coconuts, I buy very few coconuts.

TRACK 17

4. Tres tristes tigres tragaban trigo en un triste trigal.
   Three sad tigers swallowed wheat in a sad wheat field.

LESSON 3: CHAT ABOUT THE FAMILY

61 = SESENTA Y UNO

Select one of these final projects from the list. Either present these during the final lesson (#111 = ciento once) and/or share them with Hispanic employees or Spanish-speaking friends. Here are the seven final project ideas:

- **The theater = El teatro:** Roleplay a typical exchange with a Spanish speaker or a comical customer service experience. Do this alone or with a partner and use props or exaggerate to make this funny. Each person should say about 10 lines. Have a native speaker check your script before your presentation.

- **The important phrases = Las frases importantes:** Make your own list of 15 phrases you will use most. Type these in English and Spanish. (Add the pronunciation if it helps you.) Either take these from the phrases in the lessons or invent your own. Make a small "cheat sheet" to keep with you or make a poster to hang in your kitchen.

- **In the kitchen = En la cocina:** Write out at least 12 sentences in Spanish for a cooking show script. Include the steps to the recipe as you are preparing the food and the ingredients you will be using. Either videotape this cooking show to watch in two weeks or demonstrate it live.

- **The map = El mapa:** Write out at least 12 sentences that give us a tour of your home or workplace. Use directional words such as norte, sur, oeste, este, a la derecha and a la izquierda. Design this map and print it from your computer, or use a video camera and give us a walking tour in Spanish.

- **The story = El cuento:** This could be a mini-book with at least 12 sentences about any topic of your choice. It could be about Hispanic holidays, or a trip, or even a book about a typical day.

- **The travel agency = La agencia de viaje:** You are a travel agent advertising your country so people will want to come to visit. Make a brochure, poster or computer presentation about your country. See page 165 for more details and ideas about the 12 sentences required for this project.

- **Have any other ideas? = ¿Tiene alguna otra idea?:** Create any other meaningful project with at least 12-15 phrases in Spanish that will help you the most in your life.

62 = SESENTA Y DOS

Cut apart the 12 flashcards after #63 = sesenta y tres to use for "Bingo = Lotería." Choose any 16 flashcards from Lessons 1-3 and put them in any order to make four rows of 4. The "Bingo Game Board" is on the following page. Use the glossary to call out any phrases from Lessons 1-3 in any order. Flip the card over when you hear the phrase called and keep going until you have four in a row turned over. Then yell, "¡LOTERÍA!" Note: The word lotería also means lottery in some countries. You may see people walking around the streets selling these tickets, hoping their numbers will be called on a certain day of the week. In some countries the unemployed, elderly and stay-at home moms get together in the neighborhood = barrio to play "Bingo" with their spare change.

LESSON 3: CHAT ABOUT THE FAMILY

63 = SESENTA Y TRES
"BINGO = ¡LOTERÍA!" BOARD

LESSON 3: CHAT ABOUT THE FAMILY

Where do you work?	I work in a school.	What is your daughter's name?
My daughter's name is Rose.	How old are your children?	How many people are in your family?
How do you spell (write) that?	Greetings to your family.	There are ___ people in my family.
Best wishes!	Do you have animals?	My children are 11 and 13 years old.

LESSON 3: CHAT ABOUT THE FAMILY

¿Cómo se llama su hija? (KOH-moh Seh Yah-mah Soo Ee-hah?)	Trabajo en una escuela. (Trah-bah-hoh Ehn Oo-nah Ehs-kweh-lah.)	¿Dónde trabaja? (DOHN-deh Trah-bah-hah?)
¿Cuántas personas hay en su familia? (Coo/AHN-tohs Pehr-soh-nahs Eye Ehn Soo Fah-mee-lee/ah?)	¿Cuántos años tienen sus hijos? (Coo/AHN-tohs Ah-ñyohs Tee-eh-nehn Soos Ee-hohs?)	Mi hija se llama Rosa. (Mee Ee-hah Seh Yah-mah Roh-sah.)
Hay ___ personas en mi familia. (Eye ___ Pehr-soh-nahs Ehn Mee Fah-mee-lee/ah.)	Saludos a su familia. (Sah-loo-dohs Ah Soo Fah-mee-lee/ah.)	¿Cómo se escribe eso? (KOH-moh Seh Ehs-cree-beh Ehs-oh?)
Mis hijos tienen once y trece años. (Mees Ee-hohs Tee-eh-nehn Ohn-seh Ee Treh-seh Ah-ñyohs.)	¿Tiene animales? (Tee/eh-neh Ah-nee-mah-lehs?)	¡Felicidades! (Feh-lee-see-dah-dehs!)

LESSON 3: CHAT ABOUT THE FAMILY

64 = SESENTA Y CUATRO

Write the letter of the corresponding English phrase on the line next to the Spanish phrase.

1. _____ ¡Felicidades!

2. _____ ¿Cuántos años tienen sus hijos?

3. _____ Mis hijos tienen once y trece años.

4. _____ ¿Tiene animales?

5. _____ ¿Cuántos años tiene su hija?

6. _____ Mis hijos tienen cuatro y seis años.

7. _____ Trabajo en una escuela.

A. *(ah)* My children are 11 and 13 years old.

B. *(beh)* Do you have animals?

C. *(seh)* I work in a school.

D. *(deh)* How old is your daughter?

E. *(eh)* My children are 4 and 6 years old.

F. *(ehf-feh)* Best wishes!

G. *(heh)* How old are your children?

65 = SESENTA Y CINCO

You see a Hispanic mother with her children. How cute. = Que bonitos. You wonder about their ages. What would you say in Spanish? Hint: Fill in the squares of the puzzle with letters from one of the Spanish phrases from #48 = cuarenta y ocho.

LESSON 3: CHAT ABOUT THE FAMILY

66 = SESENTA Y SEIS

Translate these phrases. Write the English for the first six phrases and write the Spanish for the last six phrases. This may be done as an exam or as homework for the next lesson. When finished check your answers in the Answer Key.

1. Trabajo en una escuela. _____

2. ¿Tiene animales? _____

3. Hay ___ personas en mi familia. _____

4. Mi hija se llama Rosa. _____

5. ¿Cómo se escribe eso? _____

6. ¡Felicidades! _____

7. Where do you work? _____

8. How old are your children? _____

9. What is your daughter's name? _____

10. Greetings to your family. _____

11. My children are 11 and 13 years old. _____

12. How many people are in your family? _____

LESSON 4 LECCIÓN

WHICH WAY TO GO RELAX AND CHAT?

GOALS: In this lesson you will learn about these topics: more practice with numbers, leisure activities; adjectives and colors; giving and receiving directions; three very useful verbs: tener, querer and ir; language connections; conquistadors, why Spanish is spoken throughout the Americas, and locating South American countries: Colombia, Ecuador and Venezuela.

LESSON 4: WHICH WAY TO GO TO RELAX & CHAT

67 = SESENTA Y SIETE

Begin with the family presentations from Lesson 3. Using 51 = cincuenta y uno, tell a partner in Spanish about yourself and four family members or friends. Show your family photos as you talk about each person. Then, share three sentences about your family to the entire group. Another idea is to have each partner introduce the other person by sharing three sentences they learned about the partner's family.

68 = SESENTA Y OCHO

Try to fill out this Spanish example of the form you will get at customs = aduana. Upon your arrival, you will present the official form along with your passport. Remember, this is not the actual version, and sometimes this is called a Landing Card. The English translation for this form is in the Answer Key.

Tarjeta Internacional de Embarque/Desembarque =
International Embarkation/Disembarkation Card

_____

Nombre Completo: (Apellidos, Nombres)

_____

Fecha de Nacimiento: Día   Mes   Año

_____

Lugar de Nacimiento:

_____

Nacionalidad:

_____

Ocupación:

_____

Dirección Permanente: Calle y Número   Ciudad   Estado   Código Postal   País

Estado Civil: ☐ Soltero(a)   ☐ Casado(a)   ☐ Divorciado(a)   ☐ Viudo(a)

Motivo de Viaje: ☐ Recreo   ☐ Convención/Conferencia   ☐ Negocios
                    ☐ Estudios   ☐ Visitar Amigos y/o Parientes   ☐ Otros

_____

Firma   Fecha

LESSON 4: WHICH WAY TO GO TO RELAX & CHAT

69 = SESENTA Y NUEVE

Read aloud these three phrases about leisure activities. Use a dictionary to brainstorm other possible answers.

1. What are you going to do? =
   ¿Qué va a hacer?
   (KEH Vah Ah Ah-sehr?)

2. I'm going to watch television. =
   Voy a ver televisión.
   (Voy Ah Vehr Teh-leh-vee-see/OHN.)

3. Let's go eat. =
   Vamos a comer.
   (Vah-mohs Ah Koh-mehr.)

UN POCO MÁS = A LITTLE MORE

Ask these questions with a partner and write the partner's answers on the line provided. Spell your name using the alphabet from #58 = cincuenta y ocho.

1. ¿Cómo se llama usted? _____
2. ¿Cuál es su apellido? _____
3. ¿Cuántas personas hay en su familia? _____
4. ¿Qué va a hacer mañana? _____
5. Any other questions from Lessons 1–3. _____

70 = SETENTA

Circle the Spanish answer that best matches the Spanish question. Hint: Some of the phrases are from previous lessons.

1. ¿Cómo se llama el bebé?
   a. El bebé no llora mucho.
   b. La bebé se llama Rosita.
   c. El bebé se llama Juanito.
   d. El bebé es muy bonito.

2. ¿Qué va a hacer?
   a. Voy a ver televisión.
   b. Estoy bien.
   c. Me llamo Francisco.
   d. ¿Vas a ir al cine?

3. ¿Dónde trabaja?
   a. Voy a mi trabajo.
   b. Trabajo en un restaurante.
   c. Soy de los Estados Unidos de América.
   d. Vamos a comer.

4. ¿Cuánto cuesta?
   a. Cuesta mucho. Es caro.
   b. Cuesta $3033.
   c. No cuesta mucho. Es barato.
   d. Todos, A, B y C.

5. ¿Cuántos años tiene su hijo?
   a. Mi hija tiene 8 años.
   b. Tengo 50 años.
   c. Mi hijo tiene 10 años.
   d. Mi hijo tiene 110 años.

6. ¿Tiene animales?
   a. Tengo un perico.
   b. Tengo dos hijos.
   c. Tengo sed. (see p. 75)
   d. Tengo hambre.

7. ¿Adónde vamos mañana?
   a. Vamos al museo.
   b. Vamos a comer.
   c. Vamos a nadar.
   d. Todos, A, B y C.

8. ¿De dónde es usted?
   a. Estoy bien.
   b. Soy de Nebraska.
   c. Voy a mi clase de español.
   d. El baño está cerca.

LESSON 4: WHICH WAY TO GO TO RELAX & CHAT

71 = SETENTA Y UNO

Think back to elementary school English when the teacher explained that adjectives are words to describe nouns. One major difference between English and Spanish is the placement of the adjective. For example, in English we place the adjective in front of the noun and say, "The President lives in the White House." However, in Spanish we say, "El Presidente vive en la Casa Blanca (house white)." In Spanish you say what it is (noun) and then describe it (adjective). In Spanish the adjective follows the noun. This is the opposite of English. Another example is this: The President of Argentina lives in the pink house. = El Presidente de Argentina vive en la Casa Rosada (house pink) Read these examples aloud and then answer the five questions.

la amiga buena = the good friend (female)	las amigas buenas = the good friends (all female)
el amigo bueno = the good friend (male)	los amigos buenos = the good friends (at least one male)

Complete each sentence. Find which adjective ending matches the subject of the sentence. Remember to use the -o ending for masculine nouns and the -a ending for feminine nouns. Add the –s ending for more than one person. Then, try to make your own sentences using adjectives and colors. The Answer Key has the answers.

1. the tasty red strawberry =   la fresa ric_____ y roj_____

2. the small black ants = las hormigas negr_____ y pequeñ_____

3. the way too expensive book = el libro demasiad_____ car_____

4. the cheap but fun souvenirs = los recuerdos barat_____ pero buen_____

5. the silly but good helpers = los ayudantes tont_____ pero divertid_____

LESSON 4: WHICH WAY TO GO TO RELAX & CHAT

72 = SETENTA Y DOS

Use these five phrases to give and receive directions. Read them out loud and use the direction words at the bottom of the page.

1. Where is the bathroom? =
   ¿Dónde está el baño?
   (DOHN-deh Ehs-TAH Ehl Bah-ñyoh?)

2. How do I get to ___? =
   ¿Cómo llego a ___?
   (KOH-moh Yeh-goh Ah ___?)

3. The elevator is over there. =
   El ascensor está allá.
   (Ehl Ah-sehn-sohr Ehs-TAH Ah-YAH.)

4. Follow me over here. =
   Sígame por aquí.
   (SEE-gah-meh Pohr Ah-KEE.)

5. Excuse me. =
   Con permiso.
   (Kohn Pehr-mee-soh.)
   Note, depending on context: Excuse me. / I'm sorry. = Perdón. / Lo siento.
   (Pehr-DOHN. / Loh See/ehn-toh.)

I NEED DIRECTIONS. = NECESITO DIRECCIONES.

- turn = dobla
- right = derecha
- left = izquierda
- straight = derecho
- up = arriba
- down = abajo

- back = atrás
- front = en frente
- here = aquí/acá
- there = allí/ahí
- over there = allá
- near the = cerca de

- street = calle
- three blocks = tres cuadras
- corner = esquina
- on the first floor = en el primer piso
- on the second floor = en el segundo piso
- on the third floor = en el tercer piso

LESSON 4: WHICH WAY TO GO TO RELAX & CHAT

73 = SETENTA Y TRES

Write the letter of the corresponding English phrase on the line next to the Spanish phrase.

1. _____ Voy a ver televisión.   A. *(ah)*   Excuse me.

2. _____ ¿Cómo llego a ___?   B. *(beh)*   The elevator is over there.

3. _____ Sígame por aquí.   C. *(seh)*   Let's go eat.

4. _____ ¿Dónde está el baño?   D. *(deh)*   Follow me over here

5. _____ Con permiso.   E. *(eh)*   Where is the bathroom?

6. _____ ¿Qué va a hacer?   F. *(ehf-feh)* How do I get to ___?

7. _____ Vamos a comer.   G. *(heh)*   What are you going to do?

8. _____ El ascensor está allá.   H. *(ah-cheh)* I'm going to watch television.

74 = SETENTA Y CUATRO

If you have taken a Spanish class before, you have probably encountered verbs. Verbs are action words that are always changing—just like life. For example, in English we change "I have" to "she has." Let's look at three very useful verbs and how they change depending on the subject of the sentence. We will look at these seven subjects. For more information on the tú *(informal you)* and the vosotros = y'all form *(only used in Spain)*, buy a grammar book.

SINGULAR SUBJECT PRONOUNS:	PLURAL SUBJECT PRONOUNS:
I = Yo He = Él She = Ella You (formal) = Usted	We = Nosotros They = Ellos You all (formal, plural) = Ustedes

Read the chart out loud and then do the activities to practice with the verb.

TO HAVE = TENER:

I have. = Yo tengo.	We have. = Nosotros tenemos.
He has. = Él tiene. She has. = Ella tiene. Mary Ellen has. = María Elena tiene. You have. = Usted tiene. (formal, singular)	They have. = Ellos tienen. Anna and Francis have. = Ana y Francisco tienen. You have. = Ustedes tienen. (formal, plural)

LESSON 4: WHICH WAY TO GO TO RELAX & CHAT

75 = SETENTA Y CINCO
COMMON PHRASES USING THE VERB TENER:

Here are some typical expressions with the verb tener. "Tener sed" literally translates as, "to have thirst", but in English we say, "to be thirsty." To say, "I am thirsty", change tener by saying, "Yo tengo sed." Share two phrases with a partner.

- to be thirsty = tener sed
- to be hungry = tener hambre
- to be sleepy = tener sueño Note: tener un sueño = have a dream
- to be _____ years old = tener _____ años.
- to be cold = tener frío
- to be hot = tener calor
- to be scared = tener miedo
- to have to = tener que
- to be in a hurry = tener prisa

TO PRACTICE = PARA PRACTICAR

Fill in the blank with the correct form of the verb tener using the previous boxes to help you.

1. Yo _____ 40 años.

2. ¿_____ usted una toalla?

3. Nosotros _____ mucho trabajo.

4. Araceli _____ hambre.

5. Yo _____ frío.

6. Ellos no _____ calor.

7. Ella _____ sueño.

8. Franco _____ prisa.

9. Melchor y Carolina no _____ sed.

76 = SETENTA Y SEIS

Read the chart out loud and then do the activities to practice with the verb. Remember that these verbs are in the present tense.

TO WANT = QUERER:

I want. = Yo quiero.	We want. = Nosotros queremos.
He wants. = Él quiere. She wants. = Ella quiere. Eve wants. = Eva quiere. You want. Usted quiere. (formal)	They want. = Ellos quieren. Rose and James want. = Rosa y Santiago quieren. You want. = Ustedes quieren. (formal, plural)

Fill in the blank with the correct form of the verb querer using the previous chart to help you. Find the answers and the English translations for these sentences in the Answer Key.

1. Yo _____ ir a un restaurante.

2. Ella _____ visitar el museo.

3. ¿_____ Eduardo probar un chile relleno?

4. Catalina _____ aprender un poco español.

5. Ellos _____ tener trabajos mejores.

6. Nosotros no _____ bailar.

77 = SETENTA Y SIETE

Read the chart out loud and then do the activities to practice with the verb. This verb may also be used to talk about things that are going to happen in the future.

GOING TO = IR A:

I am going to = yo voy a	we are going to = nosotros vamos a
he is going to = él va a she is going to = ella va a Gilbert is going to = Gilberto va a you are going to = usted va a (formal, singular)	they are going to = ellos van a Ellen and John are going to = Elena y Juan van a you are going to = ustedes van a (formal, plural)

Fill in the blank with the correct form of the verb ir a using the previous chart to help you. Find the answers and the English translations for these sentences in the Answer Key.

1. Yo _____ a hacer la cena.

2. Eliana _____ a Guatemala.

3. Los clientes _____ a pagar sus cuentas.

4. Clara _____ a cambiar su ropa.

5. ¿ _____ Natalia a trabajar mañana?

6. Nosotros _____ a tener la reunión hoy.

LESSON 4: WHICH WAY TO GO TO RELAX & CHAT

78 = SETENTA Y OCHO

Read these four language connection phrases out loud. These will help you communicate with someone that you have just met.

1. Do you speak English? =
   ¿Habla inglés?
   (Ah-blah Een-GLEHS?)

2. I speak only a little Spanish. =
   Hablo un poco de español.
   (Ah-bloh Oon Poh-koh Deh Ehs-pah-ñyohl.)

3. Thank you for your patience. =
   Gracias por su paciencia.
   (Grah-see/ahs Pohr Soo Pah-see/ehn-see/ah.)

4. I would like to introduce you to ___. =
   Deseo presentarle a ___.
   (Deh-seh-oh Preh-sehn-tahr-leh Ah ___.)
   Note: Remember to say, "Mucho gusto."

79 = SETENTA Y NUEVE

Spanish is spoken throughout most of the Americas including South America. However, Portuguese is spoken in the country of Brazil. The Treaty of Tordesillas created on June 7, 1492, divided the newly discovered territory between Spain and Portugal. This treaty tried to squeeze all other European countries out of the new lands that were being discovered.

The Spanish spoken in the Americas most closely resembles the Spanish spoken in the south of Spain. This is where many of the sailors and conquistadors came from. Two famous conquistadores are Hernán Cortés, the conqueror of the Aztecs, and Francisco Pizarro, the conqueror of the Incas. There are still variations and slang words that differ in each region; for example, in Argentina, "yo me llamo" sounds like, "*Shoh Meh Shah-moh*" due to the close proximity of Portuguese spoken by neighboring Brazil. The Spanish in Argentina is also heavily influenced by the Italian immigrants that settled in Argentina.

LESSON 4: WHICH WAY TO GO TO RELAX & CHAT

80 = OCHENTA

Have one person say the lines for Shakira and the other person say the lines for Simón Bolívar. Then switch roles and present this as a skit.

Shakira:	¿Habla inglés?
Simón Bolívar:	No.
Shakira:	Yo hablo un poco de español. ¿Dónde está el baño?
Simón Bolívar:	El baño está en el segundo piso.
Shakira:	¿Dónde está el ascensor?
Simón Bolívar:	El ascensor está allá.
Shakira:	Gracias. Hasta luego y mucho gusto.
Simón Bolívar:	El gusto es mío.

Work with a partner or individually to write your own conversation or role play with a typical work situation. Include questions, problems, solutions and/or phrases from Lessons 1–4. Present this new conversation in front of the group.

81 = OCHENTA Y UNO

SOUTH AMERICA = AMÉRICA DEL SUR

To remember the Spanish-speaking countries of South America, you can use this phrase "Very Cool Extroverted Penguins Barely Participate Until Almost Chilled." In this mnemonic, the first letter of each word represents a Spanish-speaking country starting with V = Venezuela, C = Colombia, E = Ecuador, P = Peru, B = Bolivia, P = Paraguay, U = Uruguay, A = Argentina and C = Chile.

82 = OCHENTA Y DOS

Read the information about these three South American countries.

EL PAÍS	COLOMBIA	ECUADOR	VENEZUELA
LA MONEDA NACIONAL	Peso	U.S. Dollar	Bolívar
LOS LUGARES PARA VISITAR	**Santafé de Bogotá** • La Capital • Gold museum **Zipaquirá salt mine** **Cartagena** • Beachport **Tatacoa desert** **Amazon jungle**	**Quito** • La Capital **Guayaquil** **Islas Galápagos** = Galápagos Islands **Cuenca** • Cathedral Monestery **Amazon jungle**	**Caracas** • La Capital **Salto Ángel / Canaima National Park** • Waterfall • Cloud forest with 25,000 species of orchids **Isla Margarita** • Beaches
LA POBLACIÓN	47 million	16 million	30.5 million
LA GENTE FAMOSA	**Fernando Botero (Born 1932)** • Artist **Carlos Valderrama "El Pibe" (Born 1961)** • Soccer player **Shakira (Born 1977)** • Singer **Gabriel García Márquez (1927-2014)** • Nobel prize for literature **Manuel Elkin Patarroyo (Born 1946)** • Nobel prize for science, vaccine for malaria **Totó la Momposina (Born 1940)** • Singer	**Gerardo (Born 1965)** • Singer "Rico Suave" • Record Producer **Luis Miranda (Born 1932)** • Painter **Fanny Carrión de Fierro (Born 1936)** • Literature • Poet **Noralma Vera Arrata (Born 1936)** • Prima Ballerina **Rosalía Arteaga (Born 1956)** • President in 1997 for three days	**Simón Bolívar (1783–1830)** • The Great Liberator **Oscar D'Leon (Born 1943)** • Singer **Luis Aparicio (Born 1934)** • Baseball Hall of Fame **Irene Sáez (Born 1961)** • Miss Universe (1981) • Politician **Carolina Herrera (Born 1939)** • Fashion designer
LA COMIDA	**Arepa** • Thick corn tortilla **Sancocho** • Stew **Café** = Coffee • Fritanga **Grilled meats, BBQ**	**Ceviche** • Raw fish "cooked" by marinating in lemon juice, sometimes with tomato sauce **Cassava** • Yucca root **Cuy** • Fried guinea pig	**Arepa** • Bread made from corn **Pabellón Criollo** • Stewed and shredded meat with bananas, black beans and rice **Pescado y Marisco** • Fish and shellfish
EL INGRESO ANUAL = ANNUAL INCOME (GNI)	$11,960 per year	$10,720 per year	$17,900 per year

LESSON 4: WHICH WAY TO GO TO RELAX & CHAT

83 = OCHENTA Y TRES

Read these three trivia statements about Colombia, Ecuador and Venezuela. Two sentences are true and one is false. Guess which one is not true. The previous cultural section does not contain the answers, so check the Answer Key to find out why one of them is not culturally correct.

INTERESTING THINGS = COSAS INTERESANTES:

1. _____ In Zipaquirá, Colombia, the church is built entirely out of yucca roots.

2. _____ Angel Falls in Venezuela is the world's highest waterfall with a height of 3,212 feet.

3. _____ The Ecuadorian Galapágos Islands contributed to Darwin's theory of evolution.

FOOD = COMIDA:

1. _____ In Colombia, a fritanga may include grilled chicken, pig's feet, leg of lamb, blood sausage and chunchullo = fried cow intestines.

2. _____ In Venezuela, "pabellón a caballo" is stewed/shredded meat with a fried egg riding on top. "Pabellón con barandas" is made with fried plantains as side rails so the food does not fall off the plate. "Pabellón expreso" is a to-go plate.

3. _____ The cassava root (yucca) is used for making tapioca, flour, bioethanol, hay (animal feed) and ethnomedicine.

LESSON 4: WHICH WAY TO GO TO RELAX & CHAT

84 = OCHENTA Y CUATRO

Cut the flashcards on the following page apart, or make your own. Try playing the game called "Alrededor del Mundo = Around the World." The host/teacher will say the phrase in English using the flashcards from Lessons 1-5. One student will stand behind the chair of another student. These two students are competing to be the first person to correctly say the phrase in Spanish. The rest of the group will be listening and waiting patiently for their turn.

The winner is the first of the two students that is able to shout out the phrase, even if they have to look it up in their book. The rest of the group is silent. The winner now advances to the next student on the right and those two try to say the phrase in Spanish. Play continues all the way "around the room/world." The person that defeats the most opponents is declared the winner. Below is the evaluation guide for your final projects from #61 = sesenta y uno.

EVALUACIÓN DE SU PROYECTO FINAL =
FINAL PROJECT EVALUATION

CALIDAD = QUALITY (NEATNESS)
Presentation quality work

CORRECTO = CORRECT SPANISH
Correct grammar, verbs, sentences and accent marks

CREATIVIDAD = CREATIVITY
Color, Visuals and Interesting project design

PRESENTACIÓN = PRESENTATION
Loud, Clear five minute demonstration of your project

ÚTIL = USEFUL /RELEVANT
Applicable to your job and your life

VERSIÓN INICIAL = ROUGH DRAFT
Rough draft edited by either a Spanish teacher or a fluent Spanish-speaker

A TIEMPO = ON TIME
Ready at the beginning of class

TOTAL
Total percentage score out of 100

LESSON 4: WHICH WAY TO GO TO RELAX & CHAT

What are you going to do?	Let's go eat.	I'm going to watch television.
LESSON 4	LESSON 4	LESSON 4
Do you speak English?	Thank you for your patience.	I would like to introduce you to __.
LESSON 4	LESSON 4	LESSON 4
Where is the bathroom?	How do I get to ___?	Excuse me.
LESSON 4	LESSON 4	LESSON 4
Follow me over here.	The elevator is over there.	I speak only a little Spanish.
LESSON 4	LESSON 4	LESSON 4

LESSON 4: WHICH WAY TO GO TO RELAX & CHAT

Voy a ver televisión. *(Voy Ah Vehr Teh-leh-vee-see/OHN.)*	Vamos a comer. *(Vah-mohs Ah Koh-mehr.)*	¿Qué va a hacer? *(KEH Vah Ah Ah-sehr?)*
Deseo presentarle a __. *(Deh-seh-oh Preh-sehn-tahr-leh Ah ___.)*	Gracias por su paciencia. *(Grah-see/ahs Pohr Soo Pah-see/ehn-see/ah.)*	¿Habla inglés? *(Ah-blah Een-GLEHS?)*
Con permiso. *(Kohn Pehr-mee-soh.)*	¿Cómo llego a ___? *(KOH-moh Yeh-goh Ah ___?)*	¿Dónde está el baño? *(DOHN-deh Ehs-TAH Ehl Bah-ñyoh?)*
Hablo un poco de español. *(Ah-bloh Oon Poh-koh Deh Ehs-pah-ñyohl.)*	El ascensor está allá. *(Ehl Ah-sehn-sohr Ehs-TAH Ah-YAH.)*	Sígame por aquí. *(SEE-gah-meh Pohr Ah-KEE.)*

85 = OCHENTA Y CINCO

Now you have an opportunity to practice. Find these Spanish phrases in the word search and then write the English phrases on the lines. The words in each of the phrases are joined together without spaces and there are no punctuation marks. The Spanish phrases are from 72 = setenta y dos and 78 = setenta y ocho. ¡Buena suerte! = Good luck!

A	G	H	T	I	E	M	F	L	J	S	M	O	B	C
E	Ñ	T	H	A	B	L	O	A	H	O	C	R	E	M
N	D	B	U	S	C	A	P	A	L	O	B	R	C	N
E	M	I	N	G	L	É	S	R	P	I	D	O	O	A
L	G	U	S	U	T	A	L	N	U	L	I	A	N	U
R	D	E	T	I	F	H	U	K	L	M	P	O	P	J
A	A	G	R	E	S	C	M	A	S	U	E	S	E	Y
T	R	R	O	S	N	E	C	S	A	C	E	R	R	A
N	B	A	Ñ	O	R	A	D	O	R	A	C	E	M	S
E	N	C	E	P	R	E	D	E	S	C	U	A	I	O
S	I	I	A	R	L	A	H	O	R	A	T	M	S	A
E	C	A	N	E	S	P	A	Ñ	O	L	Ñ	N	O	I
R	O	S	L	B	R	A	D	L	E	R	R	A	B	L
P	C	S	Ñ	A	I	C	N	E	I	C	A	P	T	U
E	L	E	N	A	A	N	D	J	A	D	E	N	T	J

WORD SEARCH = BUSCAPALABRAS

HABLO= _____ ESPAÑOL = _____

BAÑO = _____ UN POCO = _____

CON PERMISO = _____ INGLÉS= _____

GRACIAS = _____ PACIENCIA = _____

ASCENSOR = _____ PRESENTARLE = _____

86 = OCHENTA Y SEIS

Translate these phrases. Write the English for the first six phrases and write the Spanish for the last six phrases. This may be done as an exam or as homework for the next lesson. When finished, check your answers in the Answer Key.

1. Voy a ver televisión. _____

2. Con permiso. _____

3. Deseo presentarle a __. _____

4. Vamos a comer. _____

5. Gracias por su paciencia. _____

6. El ascensor está allá. _____

7. Where is the bathroom? _____

8. I speak only a little Spanish. _____

9. How do I get to ___? _____

10. Do you speak English? _____

11. Follow me over here. _____

12. What are you going to do? _____

TIME TO SCHEDULE A CHAT

GOALS: In this lesson you will learn about these topics: telling time in Spanish, daily routine (reflexive verbs), mañana, tardiness, holidays and fiestas, months of the year/days of the week, calendar and scheduling phrases, weather, Aztec, Maya, Inca contributions, phrases for medical situations, South America; Bolivia, Perú, Chile, Argentina, Uruguay and Paraguay, the verbs "to be," and Ser versus Estar.

LESSON 5: TIME TO SCHEDULE A CHAT

87 = OCHENTA Y SIETE

To review the numbers from Lesson 2, we will play a "Bingo" game. Fill in the squares by writing the number and the Spanish word for the number. Use the number chart from #24 = veinticuatro if you need help spelling the number. After filling out all of the squares, you are ready to play. Choose one person to read the group of numbers one at a time from the Answer Key. For example, 81–90 = ochenta y uno hasta noventa. Cover the square if you have written a number between 81 and 90 in the third square on the right. If you wrote the number 95 = noventa y cinco, you will have to wait to cover the third square on the right. The first person to get four in a row, will shout, "LOTERÍA."

_____ 11–20	_____ 51–60	_____ 81–100	_____ 201–400
_____ 21–30	_____ 61–70	_____ ¿Cúantos años tiene?	_____ 401–600
_____ 31–40	_____ ¿Cúando es su cumpleaños?= When is your birthday? (Day of the month)	_____ Su número favorito = Your favorite number between 1–1,000	_____ 601–800
_____ 41–50	_____ 71–80	_____ 101–200	_____ 801–1,000

88 = OCHENTA Y OCHO

What time is it? = ¿Qué hora es? *(KEH Oh-rah Ehs?)* Using the number chart from #24 = veinticuatro, you will be able to tell time in Spanish. In traditional Spanish custom, during the first half of every hour, you add the minutes to 30. During the second half of every hour, you subtract the minutes from the next hour. With the use of cell phones the younger generation tends to simply state the hour with the exact minute.

For example:

2:00	Son las dos. This means it is 2 o'clock.
2:05	Son las dos y cinco. Y means "and," This literally means, "It is 2 o'clock and five minutes."
2:15	Son las dos y cuarto. Cu**ar**to means quarter past. Cua**tr**o means 4.
2:27	Son las dos y veintisiete.
2:30	Son las dos y media. (After 30 minutes past the hour, you have the option of subtracting from the next hour.
2:45	Son las dos cuarenta y cinco. Another way to say it is "tres menos cuarto." Menos means minus. This literally means, It's 3 minus 15 or a quarter. In other words it's 15 minutes until 3 o'clock.
2:50	Son las dos y cincuenta or tres menos diez.

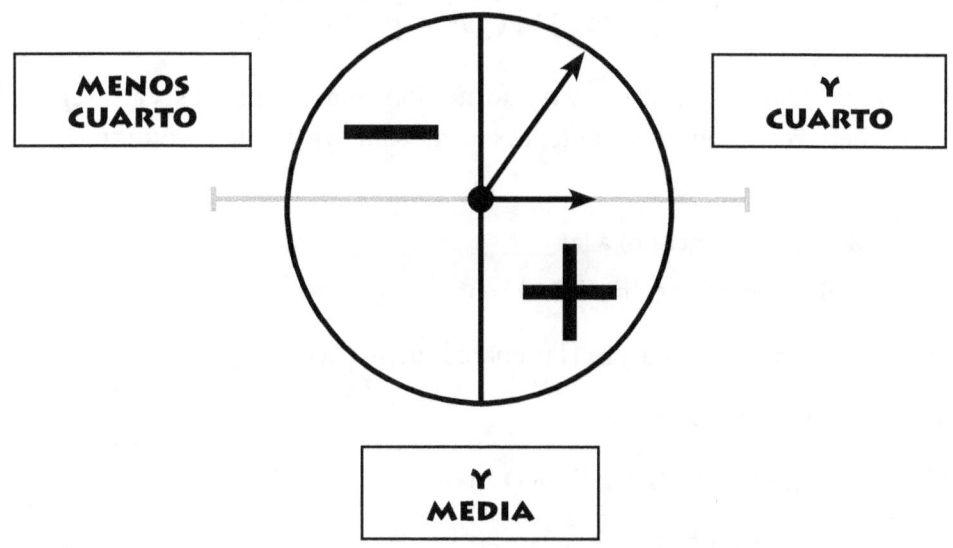

LESSON 5: TIME TO SCHEDULE A CHAT

89 = OCHENTA Y NUEVE

What is your typical day like? Fill in the blanks with the correct time.
Note: a.m. = de la mañana and p.m. = de la tarde / de la noche.

1. _____ Es la una. (Use "es" because it's the first hour/singular.)
2. _____ Son las dos. (Use "son" for the rest of the hours because they are plural.) There will be more about this in 104 = ciento cuatro.
3. _____ Son las tres.
4. _____ Son las cua**tr**o. *(Coo/ah-**tr**oh)*
5. _____ Son las cinco y cua**tr**o. *(Coo/ah-**tr**oh)*
6. _____ Son las seis y cua**rt**o. *(Coo/ah**r-to**h)*
7. _____ Son las siete y media. *(Ee Meh-dee-ah)*
8. _____ Son las ocho y media.
9. _____ Son las ocho y cuarenta OR nueve menos veinte.
10. _____ Son las nueve cuarenta y cinco OR diez menos cuarto.
11. _____ Son las diez y cincuenta OR once menos diez.
12. _____ Son las once cincuenta y cinco OR doce menos cinco.

90 = NOVENTA

Now fill in the blanks with your own information. Share the next six answers with a partner. Then create your own sentences using your typical daily routine.

13. Me levanto (I get up) a las _____
14. Yo desayuno (I eat breakfast) a las _____
15. Yo preparo el almuerzo (I prepare lunch) a las _____
16. Trabajo (I work) a las _____
17. Yo como la cena (I eat dinner) a las _____
18. Me acuesto (I go to bed) a las _____

91 = NOVENTA Y UNO

"Mañana" is one of the first words you must be familiar with when traveling or working in Latin America. It means both "tomorrow" and "morning." If someone tells you a project will get done mañana, it may be finished sometime in the future but not necessarily tomorrow. Historically, in Latin America and other parts of our world, people aren't tied to the clock. Relationships, rather than punctuality, are more of a priority. In the United States, appointments and deadlines are scheduled in advance. Tardiness is considered impolite and you may even be fired. While the culture in the United States is influencing the global marketplace in this respect, some Hispanic companies are still on their traditional schedules. For example, a bank in Spain may be closed from noon until three for a siesta every afternoon.

This relaxed attitude about time is also shown in social situations. If you are given an invitation for a party at 7 p.m., the party may actually begin around 10 p.m. Many parties = fiestas are celebrated throughout the year. A way to build rapport is to ask Hispanic friends how they are celebrating the upcoming holidays. Typical holidays and celebrations include:

- **January 6th** marks the day of the Three Kings and many Latino children have candy or other gifts placed in their shoes while they sleep.

- **Mardi Gras = Carnaval** is a celebration of parades and parties. Usually held on Fat Tuesday which is the day before Ash Wednesday. In Puerto Rico and the Dominican Republic they make elaborate masks. In Spain, groups of friends coordinate costumes and dress up in themes. For example, they might all be witches, babies or soccer players.

- **Holy Week = Semana Santa** You will find religious processions in many towns.

- **Day of the Dead = Día de los Muertos** is November 1st–2nd In México. This is essentially like Memorial Day. Families leave a trail of marigold flowers and build altars with sugar skulls to honor the deceased.

- **Independence Days** are some of the biggest celebrations in each country, with parades and festivals in the town square. For example, Independence Day in México is September 16th. (Many people confuse this with Cinco de Mayo.)

- **Cinco de Mayo** is a celebration of the victory of one Mexican/ French battle in 1862. Cinco de Mayo is actually a bigger celebration in the United States, demonstrating Mexican-American pride.

LESSON 5: TIME TO SCHEDULE A CHAT

92 = NOVENTA Y DOS

Say the months aloud using the pronunciation guide to help you.

THE MONTHS OF THE YEAR = Los meses del año:

1. January = enero *(Eh-neh-roh)*
2. February = febrero *(Feh-breh-roh)*
3. March = marzo *(Mahr-zoh)*
4. April = abril *(Ah-breel)*
5. May = mayo *(Mah-yoh)*
6. June = junio *(Who-nee/oh)*
7. July = julio *(Who-lee/oh)*
8. August = agosto *(Ah-gohs-toh)*
9. September = septiembre *(Sehp-tee/ehm-breh)*
10. October = octubre *(Oct-too-breh)*
11. November = noviembre *(Noh-vee/ehm-breh)*
12. December = diciembre *(Dee-see/ehm-breh/DCM-breh)*

UN JUEGO = A GAME

To play this game, you will need a partner and two dice. The goal is to be the first person to roll each number from 2 through 12. 2 = febrero, 3 = marzo, 4 = abril, etc. Since you are unable to roll a 1, cross off #1 January. When you roll a 4, cross off #4 April = abril from the list and say, "abril." Now pass the dice to your partner. The next time you roll a 4, you will just say abril and pass the dice to your partner, but you won't be able to cross anything off. The winner is the first person to cross off all of the numbers from 2 through 12. Another way to play is to give each person a pair of dice and have the whole group do this at the same time.

LESSON 5: TIME TO SCHEDULE A CHAT

93 = NOVENTA Y TRES

Say the days of the week aloud using the pronunciation guide to help you. Try writing your weekly schedule in Spanish.

THE DAYS OF THE WEEK = LOS DÍAS DE LA SEMANA:

- Monday = lunes *(Loo-nehs)*
  (Many calendars in Latin America start with Monday)

- Tuesday = martes *(Mahr-tehs)*

- Wednesday = miércoles *(Mee-EHR-koh-lehs)*

- Thursday = jueves *(Who/eh-vehs)*

- Friday = viernes *(Vee/ehr-nehs)*

- Saturday = sábado *(SAH-bah-doh)*

- Sunday = domingo *(Doh-mean-goh)*

LA PRÁCTICA = THE PRACTICE

Circle the English choice that matches the Spanish month.

1. **enero**
   a. June
   b. March
   c. May
   d. January

2. **octubre**
   a. September
   b. August
   c. October
   d. July

3. **jueves**
   a. Thursday
   b. Monday
   c. Saturday
   d. Sunday

4. **miércoles**
   a. Tuesday
   b. Saturday
   c. Thursday
   d. Wednesday

94 = NOVENTA Y CUATRO

Look outside and check the weather. Ask a partner what the weather is like and then listen to the answer. Use the pronunciation guide to help you.

THE WEATHER = EL CLIMA

What is the weather like today? = ¿Cómo está el clima hoy?
(KOH-moh Ehs-TAH Ehl Clee-mah Oh/ee?)

- It's windy. = Hace viento.   (Ah-seh Vee/ehn-toh.)
- It's hot. = Hace calor.   (Ah-seh Kah-lore.)
- It's sunny. = Hace sol.   (Ah-seh Sohl.)
- It's cold. = Hace frío.   (Ah-seh FREE-oh.)
- It rains. = Llueve.   (You/eh-veh.)
- It snows. = Nieva.   (Nee/eh-vah.)
- It's cloudy. = Está nublado.   (Ehs-TAH Noo-blah-doh.)

If the sun is out and you are hot, use this expression, "Yo tengo calor." Do not use, "Estoy caliente," because it would mean I am hot in a good-looking, sexual way. Along the same lines, if it's the middle of winter and you are cold, then say this phrase, "Yo tengo frío." Please do not say, "Estoy frío." Note: El tiempo means both "the time" and "the weather" depending on the context.

UN JUEGO = A GAME

In pairs play the game of charades. Take turns having one partner act out a weather word or a month of the year, and the other person will guess in Spanish. In a group, divide into teams. One person from each team would come to the front of the room to act out the word, and the rest of the team shouts out the answers. The first team to correctly guess the answer would get a point for their team.

LESSON 5: TIME TO SCHEDULE A CHAT

95 = NOVENTA Y CINCO

Calendar phrases may be used to schedule events. Ask a partner the questions and invent answers in Spanish using the months and days vocabulary from #92 = noventa y dos and #93 = noventa y tres.

1. What is the date today? =
   ¿Cuál es la fecha de hoy?
   (Coo/AHL Ehs Lah Feh-cha Deh Oh/ee?)

2. Today's date is February 13th. =
   Es el 13 de febrero.
   (Ehs Ehl Treh-seh Deh Feh-breh-roh.)

3. When is your birthday? =
   ¿Cuándo es su cumpleaños?
   (Coo/AHN-doh Ehs Soo Koom-pleh-ah-ñyohs?)

4. My birthday is June 17th. =
   Mi cumpleaños es el 17 de junio.
   (Mee Koom-pleh-ah-ñyohs Ehs Ehl Dee/eh-see-see/eh-teh Deh Who-nee/oh.)

5. What day is the appointment? =
   ¿Qué día es la cita?
   (KEH DEE-ah Ehs Lah See-tah?)

6. The appointment is Monday at 9 a.m. =
   La cita es el lunes a las 9 de la mañana.
   (Lah See-tah Ehs Ehl Loo-nehs Ah Lahs Noo/eh-veh Deh Lah Mah-ñyah-nah.)

7. What time is it? =
   ¿Qué hora es?
   (KEH Oh-rah Ehs?)

8. What is the weather like today? =
   ¿Cómo está el clima hoy?
   (KOH-moh Ehs-TAH Ehl Clee-mah Oh/ee?)

LESSON 5: TIME TO SCHEDULE A CHAT

96 = NOVENTA Y SEIS

Answer the questions below. Use the previous vocabulary to help you. The answers are in the Answer Key.

- Yesterday = Ayer *(Ah-yehr)*
- Tomorrow/Morning = Mañana *(Mah-ñyah-nah)*
- Today = Hoy *(Oh/ee)*
- The next month = El próximo mes *(Ehl PROHX-see-moh Mehs)*
- The last week = La semana pasada *(Lah Seh-mahn-nah Pah-sah-dah)*

1. Hoy es martes. ¿Ayer fue _____? (fue = was)
2. Hoy es domingo. ¿Ayer fue _____ ?
3. Hoy es miércoles. ¿Mañana será _____? (será = will be)
4. Este mes es junio. ¿El mes pasado fue _____ ?
5. Este mes es enero. ¿El próximo mes será _____ ?

AZTEC, MAYA & INCA

Before the Spaniards there were great civilizations in many countries. Here are three major native tribes and a few of their contributions.

¿QUIÉN?	AZTEC	MAYA	INCA
¿DÓNDE?	Mexico	Yucatan, Mexico and Northern Central America	Peru and South America
¿HIZO QUÉ?	• Universal education • Aztec Calendar • Popcorn • Voladores = 4 Pole flyers • Ollama = Ball game • Cochineal beetle is used for red dye • Chewing gum • Passion flower medicine • Example: Tenochtitlán Pyramid of the moon & sun	• Hot chocolate • Zero and number system with sticks and stones (#47) • Mayan Calendar • Stellas = Stone slab with Mayan codex with glyphs • Astronomy • Pitz- Hoop and rubber ball game • Dance • Headdress • Example: Tikal pyramids	• Accounting — Quipu talking knots • Roads • Brain surgery • Mummies • Mail and runner delivery system long distances • Terrace farming • Astronomical clock • Freeze dried foods • Example: Machu Picchu

LESSON 5: TIME TO SCHEDULE A CHAT

97 = NOVENTA Y SIETE

These four phrases could be used in medical situations. Read them aloud and using charades act out which part of your body is injured.

1. Watch out! =
   ¡Cuidado!
   (Coo/ee-dah-doh!) Or ¡Ojo! *(Oh-ho!)*
   Note: "¡Cuidado!" can also mean, "Be careful!" and "Caution!"

2. Do you need anything else? Do you have questions? =
   ¿Necesita algo más? ¿Tiene preguntas?
   (Neh-seh-see-tah Ahl-goh MAHS?) (Tee/eh-neh Preh-goon-tahs?)

3. Where do you hurt? =
   ¿Dónde le duele?
   (DOHN-deh Leh Dweh-leh?)

4. My hand hurts. =
   Me duele la mano.
   (Meh Dweh-leh Lah Mah-noh.)

98 = NOVENTA Y OCHO

- ankle = el tobillo
- arm = el brazo
- back = la espalda
- cough = la tos
- inner ear = el oído
- eye = el ojo
- finger = el dedo
- foot = el pie
- head = la cabeza
- knee = la rodilla
- leg = la pierna
- mouth = la boca
- neck = el cuello
- nose = la nariz
- stomach = el estómago
- throat = la garganta
- toe = el dedo del pie
- tooth = el diente / la muela
- wound = la herida
- wrist = la muñeca

LESSON 5: TIME TO SCHEDULE A CHAT

99 = NOVENTA Y NUEVE

Write the letter of the corresponding English phrase on the line next to the Spanish phrase.

1. _____ ¿Cómo está el clima hoy?

2. _____ ¿Cuándo es su cumpleaños?

3. _____ La cita es el lunes a las 9 de la mañana.

4. _____ ¡Cuidado!

5. _____ ¿Cuál es la fecha de hoy?

6. _____ Es el 13 de febrero.

7. _____ Me duele la cabeza.

8. _____ ¿Qué hora es?

9. _____ ¿Necesita algo más?

10. _____ ¿Dónde le duele?

11. _____ Mi cumpleaños es el 17 de junio.

12. _____ ¿Qué día es la cita?

A. *(ah)* Do you need anything else?

B. *(beh)* What is the date today?

C. *(seh)* When is your birthday?

D. *(deh)* What day is the appointment?

E. *(eh)* Today's date is February 13th.

F. *(ehf-feh)* What is the weather like today?

G. *(heh)* What time is it?

H. *(ah-cheh)* Where do you hurt?

I. *(eeee)* The appointment is Monday at 9 a.m.

J. *(hoh-tah)* My birthday is June 17th.

K. *(kah)* Watch out!

L. *(ehl-leh)* My head hurts.

100 = CIEN

Read the information about these three South American countries.

EL PAÍS	BOLIVIA	PERÚ	CHILE
LA MONEDA NACIONAL	Boliviano	Nuevo Sol	Peso
LOS LUGARES PARA VISITAR	**Sucre** • La Capital oficial **La Paz** • La Capital administrativa **Isla del Sol** • Island in Lake Titicaca that the Incas believe they descended from	**Lima** • La Capital • Plaza Mayor **Islas Flotantes** • Floating Islands on Lake Titicaca **Machu Picchu** • Inca Ruins **Cusco** • Inti Raymi festival **Nazca Lines** **Arequipa** • Colca Canyon	**Santiago** • La Capital • Cerro San Cristobál **San Pedro de Atacama** • Desert **Chuquicamata** • Copper mine **Easter island** • Moai stone figures **Viña del Mar/ Valparaíso** • Beach **Patagonia** • Rainforest and glaciers
LA POBLACIÓN	10.5 million	30 million	17.5 million
LA GENTE FAMOSA	**Jaime Escalante (1930-2010)** • Teacher that inspired the movie, Stand and Deliver **Marina Núñez del Prado (1910-1995)** • Sculptress **Jaime Laredo (Born 1941)** • Violinist	**Tupac Amaru II (1742–1781)** • Indigenous Leader **Mario Vargas Llosa (Born 1936)** • Nobel prize for literature in 2010 **Sofía Mulánovich (Born 1983)** • Champion Surfer **Janier Perez de Cuellar (Born 1920)** • United Nations Secretary-General (1982-1991)	**Bernardo O'Higgins (1778–1842)** • Independence Leader **Michelle Bachelet (Born 1951)** • President 2006–2010 **Pablo Neruda (1904–1973)** • Poet • Nobel Prize in Literature 1971 **Isabel Allende (Born 1942)** • Novelist
LA COMIDA	**Chicha** • Alcoholic drink made from purple corn **Humitas** • A sweet tamale **Pique Macho** • Beef, sausage, fries, boiled eggs, peppers **Salteña** • Meat/ potato pastry	**Cuy** • Roasted guinea pig **Inca Cola** • Yellow carbonated soda **Mazamorra Morada** • Purple corn pudding **Papas a la Huancaína** • Potatoes in an ají pepper, creamy sauce **Quinoa** • A nutritional grain	**Empanadas** • Triangle shaped hamburger pie usually with an olive and hard boiled egg pieces **Pastel de Choclo** • Chilean Sheppard's pie **Lúcuma /Chirimoya** • South American Fruits sometimes made into ice cream
EL INGRESO ANUAL = ANNUAL INCOME (GNI)	$3,290 per year	$11,160 per year	$21,030 per year

LESSON 5: TIME TO SCHEDULE A CHAT

101 = CIENTO UNO

Read the information about these final three South American countries.

EL PAÍS	ARGENTINA	URUGUAY	PARAGUAY
LA MONEDA NACIONAL	Peso	Peso	Guaraní
LOS LUGARES PARA VISITAR	**Buenos Aires** • La Capital • La Casa Rosada = The Pink House is the presidential palace • Plaza de Mayo • Teatro Colón • Obelisco = Obelisk **Iguazú** • Waterfalls **Pampas** • Grasslands	**Montevideo** • La Capital **Colonia de Sacramento** • Calle de los Suspiros = Oldest Street of Sighs • Portón de Campo = City Gate **Punta del Este** • Beach	**Asunción** • La Capital **Itaipú Dam** • One of the world's biggest hydroelectric dams **Chaco** • Rainforest • Butterflies **Encarnación** • Jesuit ruins
LA POBLACIÓN	42.5 million	3.5 million	6.5 million
LA GENTE FAMOSA	**Eva Perón (1919–1952)** • First Lady (1946–1952) **Diego Maradona (Born 1960)** • Soccer player **José de San Martín (1778–1850)** • Independence leader **Juan Manuel de Rosas (1793–1877)** • Ruler 1829–1852	**José Gervasio Artigas (1764–1850)** • Independence leader against Brazil and Portugal **Virginia Patrone (Born 1950)** • Painter **Natalia Oreiro (Born 1977)** • Singer, actress	**Pedro Juan Caballero (1786–1821)** • Independence figure **Francisco Solano López (1826–1870)** • Dictator and Leader of the War of Triple Alliance **Celeste Troche (Born 1981)** • Golfer
LA COMIDA	**Parrilla** • Grilled meats **Empanadas** • Pastry pockets filled with meat inside **Dulce de Leche** • Sweet, carmelized condensed milk **Dulce de Membrillo** • Quince jam **Italian Pasta Dishes**	**Asado** • Grilled meats **Chivito** • Sandwich **Alfajores** • Cookies with dulce de leche in the middle **Ñoquis/Gnocchis** • Pasta dumplings **Italian pasta dishes**	**Yerba Mate** • Tea drunk with a metal or cane straw called a "bombilla" **Tereré** • Iced herbal tea **Sopa Paraguaya** • Soup of smashed corn, cheese, milk, and onions
EL INGRESO ANUAL = ANNUAL INCOME (GNI)	$14,715 per year	$19,940 per year	$7,670 per year

SPANISH CHATBOOK

LESSON 5: TIME TO SCHEDULE A CHAT

102 = CIENTO DOS

Read these three trivia statements about Bolivia, Perú, Chile, Argentina, Uruguay and Paraguay. Two sentences are true and one is false. Guess which one is not true. Answers are in the Answer Key.

INTERESTING THINGS = COSAS INTERESANTES:

1. _____ Lake Titicaca's floating islands are made from Totora reeds that taste like celery when eaten and need to be regularly replenished. Walking on the island is like being on a bed of hay that sinks slightly. The Uros tribe lives on the islands and has an escuela flotante school.

2. _____ Chilean Poet Pablo Neruda had a carousel horse in his circular room and a cloud chair with an ocean view at his La Sebastina house.

3. _____ Uruguay has never won a World Cup in fútbol = soccer.

FOOD = COMIDA:

1. _____ Yerba Mate in Paraguay, Argentina and Uruguay is served in individual tea cups after the tea has been brewed for 24 hours.

2. _____ Cuy is roasted guinea pig served whole on the plate. This includes the little beady eyes, teeth, etc.

3. _____ Perú has 35 varieties of maize = corn and 2,000 varieties of potatoes.

THE CITY OF MACHU PICCHU

▲ MACHU PICCHU AERIAL VIEW IS SHAPED LIKE A CONDOR BIRD

103 = CIENTO TRES

Say the lines for Tupac Amaru II and Eva Perón. They are walking inside Buenos Aires and Eva bumps her head, temporarily forgetting that it is her birthday. Her party will be at the park if it is nice weather, and at the presidential palace, Pink House, if it is raining. If you have a group, have two people present this as a skit.

Tupac Amaru II:	¡Cuidado!
Eva Perón:	PUM...Ay, ay, ay.
Tupac Amaru II:	¿Dónde le duele?
Eva Perón:	Me duele la cabeza.
Tupac Amaru II:	Tome esta aspirina. ¿Necesita algo más?
Eva Perón:	Tengo una pregunta. ¿Qué día es hoy?
Tupac Amaru II:	Hoy es viernes.
Eva Perón:	¿Cuál es la fecha de hoy?
Tupac Amaru II:	Es el 7 de mayo.
Eva Perón:	Ay, no, mi cumpleaños es el 7 de mayo. ¿Qué hora es?
Tupac Amaru II:	Son las 2 de la tarde.
Eva Perón:	¡Ay de mí! Mi fiesta de cumpleaños empezó a la 1.
Tupac Amaru II:	¿Dónde es su fiesta de cumpleaños?
Eva Perón:	Es en el parque. ¿Cómo está el clima hoy?
Tupac Amaru II:	Hace frío y llueve.
Eva Perón:	Ay no. La fiesta no puede ser afuera en el parque. Tenemos que ir a la Casa Rosada. ¿Quiere venir conmigo? Vamos a llegar tarde.
Tupac Amaru II:	Por supuesto. ¡Vámonos!
Eva Perón:	¡Sí, vámonos rápido!

New words = Palabras nuevas:

PUM...Ay, ay, ay. = BOOM...Oh no.   Tome esta aspirina. = Take this aspirin.
empezó = began/started   no puede ser afuera = can't be outside
Por supuesto. = Of course.   ¡Sí, vámonos rápido! = Yes, let's go fast!
¿Quiere venir conmigo? = Do you want to go with me?   llegar tarde = arrive late

104 = CIENTO CUATRO

One of the more confusing aspects of the language for new students is the fact that there are two verbs translated as "to be." The two verbs are ser and estar. They have very specific uses.

The verb estar is used to describe temporary things like weather, health and location. Estar is also used when saying "-ing" words.

Examples: Estoy comiendo. = I am eating.
          ¿Está trabajando? = Are you working?

For most other "to be" phrases, you will use the verb ser. Ser is used to describe more permanent. Examples: She is tall. = Ella es alta. I am from Argentina. = Soy de Argentina. These things won't usually change. As you keep practicing the use of ser or estar will become natural during your conversation.

TO BE = SER OR ESTAR:

Here are two examples of the difference in meaning between ser and estar:

SER: Mi jefe es malo. = My boss is bad, as in a bad nature or character.

ESTAR: Mi jefe está malo. = My boss is feeling bad or sick.

SER: Yo soy lista. = I am smart.

ESTAR: Yo estoy lista. = I am ready.

The following pages will help you to remember when to use each verb. Keep in mind that ser is more permanent and estar is more temporary.

105 = CIENTO CINCO

START WITH CHOICE #1, SER: To help you remember when to use ser, memorize the acronym DOT COM, -the first letter of each of these six categories:

Date: Hoy es martes. = Today is Tuesday. No es el 17 de junio. = It is not June 17th.
   Es el 29 de noviembre. = It is the 29th of November.

Occupations: Él es el dueño. = He is the owner.

Time: Es la una y media. = It is 1:30. No son las once y cuarto. = It is not 11:15.

Characteristics that are permanent:
   La maestra es alta. = The female teacher is tall.
   Yo soy una mujer. = I am a woman.

Origin/Nationality:
   Chocolate es un producto de México. = Chocolate is a product from México.
   Yo soy de los EE.UU. (Estados Unidos) de América. = I am from the
          United States of America.

Mine/Possession: La receta es de Diego. = The recipe is Doug's.
   La merienda es de Rosita y Juanito. = The snack is Rosie and Johnny's.

TO BE (MORE PERMANENT) = SER:

I am. = Yo soy.	We are. = Nosotros somos.
He is. = Él es. She is. = Ella es. Adam is. = Adán es. You are. Usted es. (formal, singular)	They are. = Ellos son. Abraham and Nolan are. = Abrahán y Manolo son. You are. = Ustedes son. (formal, plural)

106 = CIENTO SEIS

CHOICE #2, ESTAR: To help you remember when to use estar, memorize the acronym WELL,- the first letter of each of these four categories:

Weather: Está nublado. = It is cloudy.

Emotion or a change from previous condition:
El maestro está cansado. = The male teacher is tired.
La gerente (jefe) está despedida. = The female manager (boss) is fired.

Locations: Usted está en la clase de español. = You are in Spanish class.

Lifestyle/Health: Yo estoy enferma. = I am sick. (female)
Yo estoy ocupado. = I am busy. (male)

To be (changing) = Estar:

I am. = Yo estoy.	We are. = Nosotros estamos.
He is. = Él está. She is. = Ella está. Michael is. = Miguel está. You are. = Usted está. (formal)	They are. = Ellos están. Cindy and Tom are. = Cintia y Tomás están. You are. = Ustedes están. (formal, plural)

Now it is time to practice the difference between ser and estar. Look carefully at the subject and meaning of each sentence and then decide if you will use ser or estar. Refer to the previous pages and charts to help you.

1. Nosotros _____ trabajando tiempo extra. (= overtime)

2. Usted _____ enojado. (= mad)

3. Nosotros _____ rubios. (= blond)

4. El presidente _____ viejo. (= old)

5. _____ las ocho y media. (= 8:30)

6. Amelia y Mateo _____ muy emocionados. (= very excited)

LESSON 5: TIME TO SCHEDULE A CHAT

107 = CIENTO SIETE

Keep working on your final projects from #61 = sesenta y uno. You will present them next time. You may want to organize a potluck fiesta for the next session. Use the recipes on pages 166-170 for ideas about what to bring. Make a sign-up sheet today to find out what everyone is bringing so you don't have too much of one thing. Don't forget the plates, silverware, drinks and napkins. Now play a game called, "Which one is the lie"? = ¿"Cuál es la mentira"? *(Coo/AHL Ehs Lah Mehn-tee-rah?)* Create three new sentences in Spanish using the vocabulary from this lesson. The trick is to write two true sentences and one false sentence. For example:

1. Tengo un libro de español. = I have a Spanish book.
2. Nosotros estamos en América del Sur. = We are in South America.
3. Quiero vacaciones. = I want a vacation/days off from work.

In this case, the second sentence would be false, unless you are lucky enough to be reading this while on vacation in South America. After you have written your sentences in both Spanish and English, then read ONLY the Spanish phrase aloud to your class or co-workers. See if they can guess which one is the lie = mentira. Choose any three from the verb list below to get started.

- Yo soy...
- Nosotros estamos...
- ¿Quiere...?
- Quiero...
- El clima es...
- Me duele...
- Voy a…
- Ellos van a...
- La fecha es...
- Mi cumpleaños es...
- Tengo...
- ¿Tiene...?

108 = CIENTO OCHO

Cut the flashcards on the following page apart, or make your own. Using your flashcards, play either "Tic-Tac-Toe" (directions from #15 = quince) or "Toma Todo" (directions from #40 = cuarenta) to further review vocabulary. Find someone outside of this group and challenge them to a game sometime this week.

LESSON 5: TIME TO SCHEDULE A CHAT

What is the date today?	Today's date is February 13th.	When is your birthday?
My birthday is June 17th.	What day is the appointment?	The appointment is Monday at 9 a.m.
What time is it?	What is the weather like today?	Where do you hurt?
My hand hurts.	Watch out!	Do you need anything else? Do you have questions?

LESSON 5: TIME TO SCHEDULE A CHAT

¿Cuándo es su cumpleaños? *(Coo/AHN-doh Ehs Soo Koom-pleh-ah-ñyohs?)*	Es el 13 de febrero. *(Ehs Ehl Treh-seh Deh Feh-breh-roh.)*	¿Cuál es la fecha de hoy? *(Coo/AHL Ehs Lah Feh-cha Deh Oh/ee?)*
La cita es el lunes a las 9 de la mañana. *(Lah See-tah Ehs Ehl Loo-nehs Ah Lahs Noo/eh-veh Deh Lah Mah-ñyah-nah.)*	¿Qué día es la cita? *(KEH DEE-ah Ehs Lah See-tah?)*	Mi cumpleaños es el 17 de junio. *(Me Koom-pleh-ah-ñyohs Ehs Ehl Dee/eh-see-see/eh-teh Deh Who-nee/oh.)*
¿Dónde le duele? *(DOHN-deh Leh Dweh-leh?)*	¿Cómo está el clima hoy? *(KOH-moh Ehs-TAH Ehl Clee-mah Oh/ee?)*	¿Qué hora es? *(KEH Oh-rah Ehs?)*
¿Necesita algo más? *(Neh-seh-see-tah Ahl-goh MAHS?)* ¿Tiene preguntas? *(Tee/eh-neh Preh-goon-tahs?)*	¡Cuidado! *(Coo/ee-dah-doh!)* ¡Ojo! *(Oh-ho!)*	Me duele la mano. *(Meh Dweh-leh Lah Mah-noh.)*

109 = CIENTO NUEVE

Complete the crossword puzzle with words from the 12 Spanish phrases from #99 = noventa y nueve. There are no punctuation marks or spaces between words. Find the opposite translation. If the clue is in Spanish, then write the English phrase. If the clue is in English, then write the Spanish phrase. Check your answers in the Answer Key.

VERTICAL
1 CUIDADO
4 DÍAS
5 ABRIL
6 CLIMA
8 DUELE
11 OJO

HORIZONTAL
2 ANYTHING ELSE
3 WHEN
7 BIRTHDAY
9 TODAY
10 QUESTIONS
12 DO YOU NEED

LESSON 5: TIME TO SCHEDULE A CHAT

110 = CIENTO DIEZ

Translate these phrases. Write the English for the first six phrases and write the Spanish for the last seven phrases. This may be done as an exam or as homework for the next lesson.

1. ¿Dónde le duele? _____

2. Es el 13 de febrero. _____

3. ¡Cuidado! _____

4. La cita es el lunes a las 9 de la mañana. _____

5. ¿Qué hora es? _____

6. ¿Tiene preguntas? _____

7. What is the date today? _____

8. My hand hurts. _____

9. When is your birthday? _____
   _____

10. My birthday is June 17th. _____
    _____

11. What is the weather like today? _____
    _____

12. What day is the appointment? _____

13. Do you need anything else? _____

LESSON 6 LECCIÓN

Chatting at the Restaurant

GOALS: In this lesson you will learn about these: menus and Latin American schedules, restaurant and beginning of the meal phrases, communication styles, Puerto Rico, Dominican Republic, Cuba and Equatorial Guinea, end of the meal restaurant phrases, travel advice, regular present tense –ar, -er, and -ir verb conjugation, 10 ideas to continue learning in the future, grocery store scavenger hunt and field trip, and your certificate of completion.

LESSON 6: CHATTING AT THE RESTAURANT

111 = CIENTO ONCE

Now that it is the final lesson, it is time to share your projects explained in #61 = sesenta y uno enjoy your food fiesta that was described in #107 = ciento siete. Present these final projects in front of the group and/or share them with your Hispanic employees. If you have time, use the flash cards from the previous lessons and play a trivia/vocabulary game. Divide the group into two teams and choose one person to go first from each team or play this with partners. Someone will announce a phrase in English. Use the phrases on the flashcards or ask trivia questions about the 21 Spanish-speaking countries covered throughout the book. The first person to give the correct answer in Spanish gets a point. The winner is the person or the team that gets the most points at the end of 10 minutes. Use the Glossary for phrases. ¡Buena suerte! = Good luck!

112 = CIENTO DOCE

Read the paragraph silently to yourself and then have each person read one sentence aloud. Finally, answer the four questions to check your understanding. Look in the Answer Key, for an English translation of the paragraph and to check your answers.

Durante el verano, mi familia va a ir a San Juan, Puerto Rico. Hay muchos restaurantes, iglesias, museos, edificios y gente. Hay casi 1.6 millones de habitantes en el área de la capital. Vamos a ver El Castillo de San Felipe del Morro y el bosque tropical lluvioso El Yunque. Queremos comer tostones, frijoles y arroz con pollo y beber piraguas. Finalmente, vamos a relajarnos en la playa.

Using the previous paragraph, answer these four questions about the family's summer vacation last year.

1. Where is the family going to go this summer? _____
2. How big is the population in the capital? _____
3. What two tourist attractions will they go to see? _____
4. What do they want to eat? _____

113 = CIENTO TRECE

Ready to go out to eat? Make a sample menu with some of your favorite food items or translate the menu from your favorite restaurant. Below are a few ideas to get you started, for more food words use your favorite Spanish/English dictionary.

THE FOODS = LAS COMIDAS	THE DRINKS = LAS BEBIDAS
1. Bistec	1. Vaso de agua con gas
2. Hamburguesa con queso	2. Café con leche
3. Papas fritas	3. Refresco
4. Arroz con pollo	4. Botella de vino tinto
5. Ensalada y frutas frescas	5. Cerveza

Eating times and schedules vary in Latin America. Many businesses, museums and schools don't start until 9:00 a.m. The biggest difference is lunch = almuerzo. The main meal = la comida is eaten generally around 2:00 p.m. and consists of many courses. In fact, some shops and schools set their schedules around this meal so entire families can eat together. In some schools in Spain the children eat breakfast = desayuno and then go to school from 9:00 a.m. to 12:00 noon. After a three hour lunch break school resumes from 3:00 to 5:00 p.m. After school and work, a light snack = merienda is eaten.

Many Americans have been caught by surprise when restaurants are closed around 5:00 or 6:00 p.m. since no one is eating "supper" at that time. The last meal of the day is generally a light sandwich supper = cena around 9:00 or 10:00 at night. Generally people stay up much later in Latin American countries than in the United States, and parties last all night. For example, a wedding in Costa Rica had a timetable of 7:00 p.m. for the church service. At 8:00 p.m. the dancing at the reception started. The food was served at 10:00 p.m. The reception lasted until 5:00 a.m.!

LESSON 6: CHATTING AT THE RESTAURANT

114 = CIENTO CATORCE

Practice these six Spanish phrases to use at restaurants. These will help you with ordering at the beginning of the meal and #119 ciento diecinueve will have more phrases for during and after the meal. Does talking about food make you hungry? Are you thirsty for a drink?

1. Welcome. Thank you for coming. =
   Bienvenidos. Gracias por venir.
   (Bee/ehn-veh-nee-dohs.) (Grah-see/ahs Pohr Veh-neer.)
   Note: You could also say; We appreciate your visit. =
   Agradecemos su visita.
   (Ah-grah-deh-seh-mohs Soo Vee-see-tah.)

2. I am hungry. I am thirsty. =
   Tengo hambre. Tengo sed.
   (Tehn-goh Ahm-breh.) (Tehn-goh Sehd.)

3. What would you like? =
   ¿Qué le gustaría?
   (KEH Leh Goose-tah-REE/ah?)

4. I would like to order coffee. =
   Me gustaría pedir un café.
   (Meh Goose-tah-REE/ah Peh-deer Oon Kah-FEH.)

5. What do you recommend? =
   ¿Qué es lo que recomienda?
   (KEH Ehs Loh Keh Reh-koh-mee/ehn-dah?)

6. What is your favorite food or drink? =
   ¿Cuál es su comida o bebida favorita?
   (Coo/AHL Ehs Sue Koh-mee-dah Oh Beh-bee-dah Fah-voh-ree-tah?)

SPANISH CHATBOOK 1 © SPANISH CHAT COMPANY

LESSON 6: CHATTING AT THE RESTAURANT

115 = CIENTO QUINCE

Have two people say the lines for Luisa Capetillo and Roberto Clemente. Then switch roles.

Luisa Capetillo:	¿Qué va a hacer?
Roberto Clemente :	Voy a ver televisión.
Luisa Capetillo:	Pero, tengo hambre y tengo sed.
Roberto Clemente :	Bueno. ¿Le gusta la comida del restaurante "La Estancia"?
Luisa Capetillo:	Sí, me encanta. Es muy rica.
Roberto Clemente :	¿Qué es lo que recomienda?
Luisa Capetillo:	Recomiendo la parrilla. = grilled meats
Roberto Clemente :	¡Vamos! Voy a ver televisión y después al restaurante.

116 = CIENTO DIECISÉIS

Circle the English choice that matches the Spanish phrase.

1. **Cuesta 16 dólares.**
   a. It takes 16 hours.
   b. It costs 16 dollars.
   c. She is 16 years old.
   d. We have 16 doors.

2. **¿Cuánto cuesta el plato del día?**
   a. How many plates broke today?
   b. How many plates did you use today?
   c. What is on the plate of the day menu?
   d. How much does the plate of the day cost?

3. **Quiero pedir las tortillas de harina.**
   a. I want more corn tortillas.
   b. I want more tortilla omelette.
   c. Here are your flour tortillas.
   d. I want to order the flour tortillas.

4. **Yo le recomiendo mi plato favorito.**
   a. I recommend my favorite dish.
   b. I don't recommend any dishes here.
   c. This is my favorite dish.
   d. I recommend my favorite steak.

5. **¿Qué le gustaría pedir para comer?**
   a. When would you like to come over?
   b. What would you like to order to eat?
   c. Would you like to eat crickets?
   d. What would you like to drink?

6. **Bienvenidos a nuestro restaurante.**
   a. Welcome to our world.
   b. This is a great restaurant.
   c. Welcome to our restaurant.
   d. Come back again to our restaurant.

LESSON 6: CHATTING AT THE RESTAURANT

117 = CIENTO DIECISIETE

You would like to find a good restaurant in the area. You ask at the front desk of the hotel, "What is your favorite restaurant?" Fill in the squares of the puzzle with a new Spanish phrase combining words from the previous pages in this lesson. Check your answer in the Answer Key.

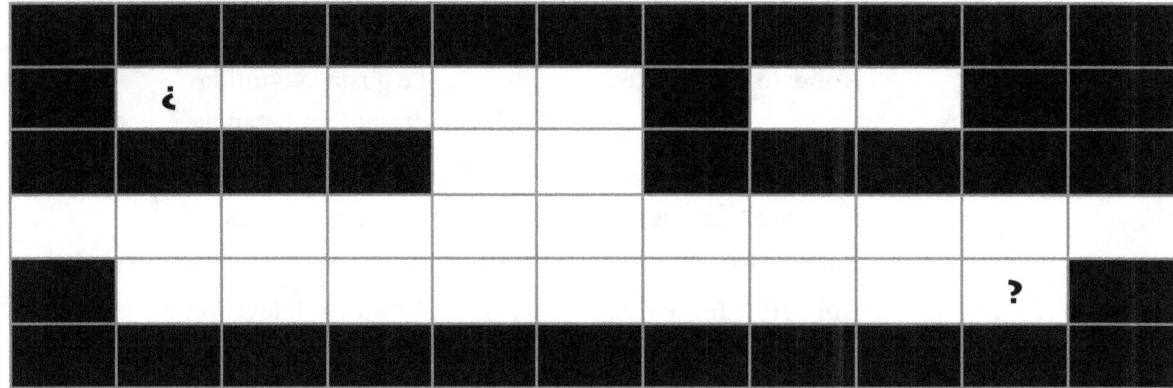

118 = CIENTO DIECIOCHO

Communication styles vary in different cultures. For example, a bilingual worker, Juanito, may spend time a great deal of time talking with someone that is interested in learning Spanish. Juanito would feel rude if he tried to rush the person and get back to his tasks, even if there was a lot of work to be done. Many people in the United States are known for accomplishing goals even at the cost of being very direct and blunt. Other cultures stereotype this attitude as the "Ugly American."

Latino culture is similar to other cultures around the world in that it is very important to save face and cooperate with other people. However, this causes Latinos to often say "yes" when they really mean "no." Latino employees generally will open up and tell you what they really mean only after they get to know you. Keeping this in mind, supervisors may want to ask individuals if anything is bothering them instead of waiting for someone to speak up in front of a group.

119 = CIENTO DIECINUEVE

Try out these six restaurant phrases while you're eating or at the end of the meal at your favorite restaurant.

1. Cheers! Enjoy your meal. (Bon appétit.) =
   ¡Salud! Buen provecho.
   (Sah-lood!) (Bwhen Proh-veh-cho.)

2. Do you like the food? =
   ¿Le gusta la comida?
   (Leh Goose-tah Lah Koh-mee-dah?)

3. Yes, I love it. It's delicious. =
   Sí, me encanta. Es muy rica.
   (SEE, Meh Ehn-kahn-tah.) (Ehs Moo/ee Ree-kah.)

4. Is everything O.K.? =
   ¿Está todo bien?
   (Ehs-TAH Toh-doh Bee/ehn?)

5. The bill, please. =
   La cuenta, por favor.
   (Lah Coo/ehn-tah, Pohr Fah-vohr.)

6. I enjoyed myself very much. =
   Me he divertido mucho.
   (Meh Eh Dee-vehr-tee-doh Moo-cho.)

OTHER USEFUL DINING TERMS

I need... = Necesito...

a plate = un plato
a fork = un tenedor
a napkin = una servilleta
a spoon = una cuchara
a knife = un cuchillo
a glass = un vaso

LESSON 6: CHATTING AT THE RESTAURANT

120 = CIENTO VEINTE

Read the information about these three islands and one Spanish-speaking country in Africa.

EL PAÍS	PUERTO RICO	DOMINICAN REPUBLIC	CUBA	EQUATORIAL GUINEA
LA MONEDA NACIONAL	U.S. Dollar	Dominican Peso	Cuban Peso	Franc
LOS LUGARES PARA VISITAR	San Juan • *La Capital* El Moro • *The fortress* Las Cuevas de Camuy El Yunque • *National park* • *Rainforest*	Santo Domingo • *La Capital* Las playas • *1,000 miles of white sand beaches* Tres Ojos de Agua • *Caves* Amber coast	Havana • *La Capital* • *Forteleza = Fortress* • *Castillos = Castles* • *Gran Teatro* • *National Ballet*	Malabo • *La Capital* • *This former Spanish colony in Africa gained independence in 1968*
LA POBLACIÓN	3.5 million	10.5 million	11 million	757,000
LA GENTE FAMOSA	Ricky Martin (Born 1971) • *Singer* Roberto Clemente (1934–1972) • *Baseball Player* Luisa Capetillo (1879–1922) • *Labor activist, women's rights*	Juan Pablo Duarte (1813–1876) • *Founding Father of the Republic* Julia Alvarez (Born 1950) • *Author* David Ortiz "Big Papi" (Born 1975) • *Baseball player*	Celia Cruz (1925–2003) • *Singer* Fidel Castro (1926–2016) • *Dictator (1959–2008)* José Martí (1853–1895) • *Poet* • *Writer* Albita Rodriguez (Born 1962) • *Singer*	Obiang Nguema (Born 1942) • *Began as dictator (1979-present)* Equatorial Guinea Women's National Soccer Team • *Hosted and won the 2008 Women's Aftrican Football Championship*
LA COMIDA	Frijoles Negros • *Black bean Soup* Arroz con Pollo • *Chicken and rice* Tostones • *Twice fried plantains*	Dominican Sancocho • *Stew* Mangú • *Mashed plantain*	Tostones • *Twice fried plantains* Frijoles Negros • *Black beans* Sandwich Cubano • *Pork, ham and cheese sandwich*	Arroz • *Rice* Pescado • *Fish* Malamba • *Drink made from sugarcane* Cassava • *Yucca*
EL INGRESO ANUAL = ANNUAL INCOME	$23,840 per year	$9,690 per year	$18,520 per year	$23,270 per year

121 = CIENTO VEINTIUNO

Read these three trivia statements about Puerto Rico, Dominican Republic, Cuba and Equatorial Guinea. Two sentences are true and one is false. Guess which one is not true. The previous cultural section does not contain the answers, so check the Answer Key to find out why one of them is not culturally correct.

INTERESTING THINGS = COSAS INTERESANTES:

1. _____ When you swim at night in the Bioluminescence Bay in Puerto Rico, the organisms light up as you move in the water.

2. _____ Yank tanks are classic cars in Cuba. Many were purchased from the U.S. before the 1959 embargo and are still running.

3. _____ Equatorial Guinea is located just north of Brazil.

FOOD = COMIDA:

1. _____ In the Dominican Republic, la bandera = the flag is a lunch of rice, red beans, plantains, meat and salad.

2. _____ In Puerto Rico, tostones are plantains that are usually toasted in a toaster oven.

3. _____ In Cuba, Ropa Vieja = Old clothes is a delicious meal of shredded steak in tomato sauce, black beans, yellow rice, fried yucca and plantains.

- A great way to increase your level of Spanish is to find a native speaker and meet weekly for an "intercambio" or "exchange." Speak English for half of the time and Spanish for the other half. This will help you to increase your skills and practice the language during real conversations.

- When meeting people from different Spanish-speaking countries it may be fun to write down and practice their unique slang expressions.

- Use a small notebook to make your own personal dictionary of your favorite phrases from this book and new words from native speakers. Writing these down is a great way to practice and retain new vocabulary.

LESSON 6: CHATTING AT THE RESTAURANT

122 = CIENTO VEINTIDÓS

Write the letter of the corresponding English phrase on the line next to the Spanish phrase.

1. _____ Tengo hambre y sed.

2. _____ ¿Qué le gustaría?

3. _____ ¿Cuál es su comida o bebida favorita?

4. _____ Gracias por venir.

5. _____ ¡Salud!

6. _____ Me he divertido mucho.

7. _____ Sí me encanta, es muy rica.

8. _____ ¿Qué es lo que recomienda?

9. _____ La cuenta, por favor.

10. _____ Me gustaría pedir un café.

11. _____ ¿Le gusta la comida?

12. _____ Bienvenidos.

13. _____ Buen provecho.

14. _____ ¿Está todo bien?

A. *(ah)*   I enjoyed myself very much.

B. *(beh)*   Thank you for coming.

C. *(seh)*   Cheers!

D. *(deh)*   What do you recommend?

E. *(eh)*   Is everything O.K.?

F. *(ehf-feh)*   What is your favorite food or drink?

G. *(heh)*   What would you like?

H. *(ah-cheh)*   I would like to order coffee.

I. *(eeee)*   Bon Appétit.

J. *(hoh-tah)*   I am hungry and thirsty.

K. *(kah)*   Yes, I love it. It's delicious.

L. *(ehl-leh)*   Welcome.

M. *(ehm-meh)*   Do you like the food?

N. *(ehn-neh)*   The bill, please.

123 = CIENTO VEINTITRÉS

After you have learned all these phrases, it is time to take a vacation. Here is some travel advice. When traveling, it is important to make sure your passport is protected at all times. This is the document that is the key for entering and leaving any country.

Before you leave, make copies of all important documents; leave a copy at home with a trusted friend and carry a copy in your suitcase. If something is lost or stolen, this copy will come in handy. Invest in a good travel wallet, which is like a pouch. These may be concealed under your clothes and hide items like a passport, credit cards, ATM cards and money. Fanny packs and back packs may be easily compromised by a determined thief. It may be a good idea to leave your jewelry and rings at home as they are not needed and will attract the wrong people.

Latin America is very enjoyable provided you don't forget to pack your common sense. The main thing is to enjoy yourself and be willing to practice your newly acquired Spanish. La práctica hace al maestro. = Practice makes perfect. Also remember to take a break. After all, you are on vacation!

124 = CIENTO VEINTICUATRO

In Spanish there are roughly 10,000 verbs. The breakdown is about 9,000 verbs ending in the letters –ar. There are about 500 –er verbs and 500–ir verbs. In English and in Spanish, verbs must be matched with their subject. An English example is the verb to be. In English we say, "I am," "you are," and "he is." Some English verbs barely change when matching to their subject. Examples: "I speak." "He speaks." There isn't a lot of difference between speak and speaks. In our native language of English we conjugate without much thought.

However, as many people have taken high school Spanish may attest, you have to conjugate, conjugate and conjugate some more to pass the class. In this lesson we will begin with present tense verbs. The purpose of this next exercise is to show the basics of conjugation so you can further your knowledge on your own. If you don't understand it, don't worry. We won't tell your high school teacher.

125 = CIENTO VEINTICINCO

PRESENT TENSE -AR VERBS:

To conjugate and change these verbs to match the subject, take off the -ar, - er or -ir then add the correct ending. Read the chart out loud and then do the activities to practice with the verb. For example, for the verb "cantar = to sing;" Andrew sings = Andrés canta. Now if Andrew's sister Emily begins singing, you will use the plural (ellos, ellas, ustedes) form and say Andrew and Emily sing = Andrés y Emilia cantan.

TO SPEAK = HABLAR (-AR):

SINGULAR	PLURAL
I speak. = Yo hablo. Add -o	We speak. = Nosotros hablamos. Add –amos
He speaks. = Él habla. Add -a She speaks. = Ella habla. Add -a You speak. = Usted habla. Add -a (Usted is the formal you.)	They speak. = Ellos hablan. (Ellos = Masculine) Add -an They speak. = Ellas hablan. (Ellas = Feminine) Add -an You speak. = Ustedes hablan. Add -an (Ustedes is you plural and formal. Vosotros is used in Spain.)

(-ER) AND (-IR) VERB FOLLOW THE SAME PATTERN:

yo - o	nosotros - emos OR -imos
él - e ella - e usted - e	ellos - en ellas - en ustedes - en

LESSON 6: CHATTING AT THE RESTAURANT

126 = CIENTO VEINTISÉIS

Step by step you will get better at Spanish, but you have to keep practicing. Fill out the endings for these verbs and check the answers.

1. **COCINAR = TO COOK**
   Yo _____
   Usted _____
   Ellos _____

2. **TRABAJAR = TO WORK**
   El bebé no _____
   Mateo y yo (nosotros) _____
   Ellos _____

3. **COMER = TO EAT**
   Yo _____
   Ella _____
   Carina y Miguel _____

4. **ASISTIR = TO ATTEND**
   Yo _____
   Nosotros _____
   Ellas _____

127 = CIENTO VEINTISIETE

To play this game, roll one die and conjugate the verb on that line. Then pass the die to your partner who will roll to conjugate a verb on their own paper. Alternate turns. If you already have that verb filled in, you will have to pass the die to your partner without conjugating. The first person to roll all six numbers and be the first one to conjugate all six verbs correctly wins. Answers are in the Answer Key.

If you roll a 1:	Yo _____.	to wash = lavar
If you roll a 2	Ella _____.	to arrive = llegar
If you roll a 3	Él _____.	to learn = aprender
If you roll a 4	Usted _____.	to read = leer
If you roll a 5	Nosotros _____.	to live = vivir
If you roll a 6	Ellos _____.	to open = abrir

LESSON 6: CHATTING AT THE RESTAURANT

128 = CIENTO VEINTIOCHO

A CONVERSATION = UNA CONVERSACIÓN

Now that you have learned some phrases, it is time to create your own conversations. Finish the following sentences using any Spanish resources to help you. The English translation is in the Answer Key. If you have a group, you can all share #1, then present #2...as time allows.

1. Me gusta _____
2. No me gusta _____
3. Yo soy _____
4. Yo estoy _____
5. Algún día, voy a... (a dream = un sueño) _____
6. Quiero tener _____
7. Mi comida favorita es _____
8. Mi trabajo es _____
9. Necesito _____
10. Aquí nadie sabe, pero en el pasado yo _____
    _____
11. Quisiera conocer (a person = una persona) _____
12. Este verano voy a _____
13. Nunca puedo _____
14. ¿Un viaje gratis? ¡Perfecto! Voy a _____
    (with who? = ¿con quién?) con _____

A GAME = UN JUEGO

Cut apart the 12 flashcards on the following page to use for "Bingo= Lotería." Combine with any 16 flashcards from Lessons 1-6 and put them in any order to make four rows of 4. Use the phrases from the glossary to call out the phrases. Flip the card over when you hear the phrase called and keep going until you have four in a row turned over. Then yell, "¡LOTERÍA!"= "BINGO." You can use the "Bingo Game Board" on #63 = sesenta y tres. Another idea is to separate all of the flashcards with questions from Lessons 1-6. Use these question cards to interview Spanish-speaking friends and brainstorm possible answers.

LESSON 6: CHATTING AT THE RESTAURANT

I am hungry. I am thirsty. LESSON 6	What would you like? LESSON 6	I would like to order coffee. LESSON 6
What do you recommend? LESSON 6	What is your favorite food or drink? LESSON 6	The bill, please. LESSON 6
Welcome. Thank you for coming. LESSON 6	I enjoyed myself very much. LESSON 6	Cheers! Enjoy your meal. LESSON 6
Do you like the food? LESSON 6	Is everything O.K.? LESSON 6	Yes, I love it. It's delicious. LESSON 6

LESSON 6: CHATTING AT THE RESTAURANT

Me gustaría pedir un café. *(Meh Goose-tah-REE/ah Peh-deer Oon Kah-FEH.)*	¿Qué le gustaría? *(KEH Leh Goose-tah-REE/ah?)*	Tengo hambre. *(Tehn-goh Ahm-breh.)* Tengo sed. *(Tehn-goh Sehd.)*
La cuenta, por favor. *(Lah Coo/ehn-tah, Pohr Fah-vohr.)*	¿Cuál es su comida o bebida favorita? *(Coo/AHL Ehs Soo Koh-mee-dah Oh Beh-bee-dah Fah-voh-ree-tah?)*	¿Qué es lo que recomienda? *(KEH Ehs Loh KEH Reh-koh-mee-ehn-dah?)*
¡Salud! *(Sah-lood!)* Buen provecho. *(Bwhen Proh-veh-cho.)*	Me he divertido mucho. *(Meh Eh Dee-vehr-tee-doh Moo-cho.)*	Bienvenidos. *(Bee/ehn-veh-nee-dohs.)* Gracias por venir. *(Grah-see/ahs Pohr Veh-neer.)*
Sí, me encanta. *(SEE, Meh Ehn-kahn-tah.)* Es muy rica. *(Ehs Moo/ee Ree-kah.)*	¿Está todo bien? *(Ehs-TAH Toh-doh Bee/ehn?)*	¿Le gusta la comida? *(Leh Goose-tah Lah Koh-mee-dah?)*

SPANISH CHATBOOK ❶ © SPANISH CHAT COMPANY

LESSON 6: CHATTING AT THE RESTAURANT

129 = CIENTO VEINTINUEVE

Now that you have made it to the final lesson of the book, the question is, "How do you continue the learning?" The most important thing is to practice, practice, practice. Here are 10 suggestions to keep yourself and others enthusiastic about learning the language.

1. **STUDY = ESTUDIA:** Keep your study materials handy and use them often. Customize phrase lists and laminate them to post on your refrigerator or at your work area. Practice games with your flashcards.

2. **TALK = HABLA:** Create opportunities for speaking Spanish. Ask native speakers questions in Spanish and learn the appropriate response. Learn a new phrase a day.

3. **THE CLASSES = LAS CLASES:** Attend refresher lessons. Not everybody is able to master the material during a 6-week lesson. Sign up for an online class or una clase at your local university. Try the *Spanish Chatbook 2* for more conversational practice with key verbs.

4. **A LUNCH IN SPANISH. = UN ALMUERZO EN ESPAÑOL:** Organize a lunch led by a Spanish speaker. Speak in Spanish about your interests, current events, or what is happening in your life. Meet the first Friday of each month to chat in Spanish.

5. **A SPECIAL DAY = UN DÍA ESPECIAL:** Choose a day and incorporate Spanish as much as possible. Plan a specific day to practice your phrases. Greet others and ask questions in Spanish.

6. **FRIENDS = AMIGOS:** Look for a native speaker who would like to help you speak Spanish and practice together often. Find someone online to chat with in Spanish who actually lives in Latin America.

7. **THE LATIN LIFE = LA VIDA LATINA:** Bring in Spanish music with the English translations and learn some popular songs. Listen to a Spanish radio station in the car, or watch a Spanish TV channel. Look up the news online and read newspapers from all over Latin America.

8. **THE CULTURE = LA CULTURA:** There is a lot of diversity in the Spanish-speaking world. Find Hispanic cultural activities nearby, visit travel Web sites or spend a week at a language school in Latin America.

9. **SEARCH = BÚSQUEDA:** Utilize the scavenger hunt/field trip form. Buy five new items from a grocery store that has Hispanic products.

10. **TRY IT! = ¡INTÉNTELO!:** Try out your new skills and continue to communicate in Spanish. Finally, remember "Donde existe voluntad, hay un camino. = Where there is a will, there is a way."

LESSON 6: CHATTING AT THE RESTAURANT

130 = CIENTO TREINTA

Translate these phrases. Write the English for the first six phrases and write the Spanish for the last six phrases. This may be done as an exam or as homework for the next lesson. When finished, check your answers in the Answer Key.

1. ¡Salud! Buen provecho. _____

2. ¿Cuál es su comida o bebida favorita? _____

3. Tengo hambre y sed. _____

4. Me gustaría pedir un café. _____

5. ¿Le gusta la comida? _____

6. Me he divertido mucho. _____

7. The bill, please. _____

8. What would you like? _____

9. Is everything O.K.? _____

10. Welcome. Thank you for coming. _____

11. Yes, I love it. It's delicious. _____

12. What do you recommend? _____

LESSON 6: CHATTING AT THE RESTAURANT

131 = CIENTO TREINTA Y UNO

Take this paper to the grocery store in your town with the most Mexican/Latin American products. If you do not find all of the items at the store, search the Internet to answer the questions. See how many of these Spanish questions you understand, before you look at the English version that follows.

EL SUPERMERCADO: _____

LAS FRUTAS Y LAS VERDURAS:

1. ¿De qué color son los nopales? Rojos o Verdes o Cafés _____

2. ¿Cómo se llaman algunos tipos de chiles? Se llaman chiles anchos, chiles _____ , chiles _____ .

3. ¿Cuánto cuesta una yuca? Una yuca cuesta $ _____ .

4. Los plátanos no son bananas. ¿Cuántos plátanos hay? **Muchos o Pocos**

5. ¿Cuánto cuesta alguna otra verdura o fruta de América Latina?
   _____ cuesta $_____ .
   (name of item = nombre)   (price = precio)

LOS DULCES:

6. ¿La marca del chocolate caliente es Abuelita o Mamá? _____

7. ¿Cuáles son los sabores de dos refrescos, gaseosas o jugos? Por ejemplo, los sabores son piña, tamarindo, _____ y _____.

8. ¿Cómo se llama un dulce de México? Se llama _____.

9. ¿Cúales son los tres tipos de papas o galletas. Los tipos son
   _____, _____ y_____.

LESSON 6: CHATTING AT THE RESTAURANT

132 = CIENTO TREINTA Y DOS

LA COMIDA TÍPICA:

10. ¿Cuáles son tres ingredientes en un mole? Los ingredientes son _____ y _____ y _____.

11. ¿Cuál es el símbolo del "Pan Bimbo?" _____

12. ¿Cuánto cuesta la harina preparada para tortillas o masa instantánea de maíz? Cuesta $_____.

13. ¿Cuántas marcas de frijoles refritos hay? Hay #_____ marcas.

14. ¿Cúal es la diferencia entre tortillas y tostadas? _____

LAS OTRAS COSAS:

15. ¿Cómo se llaman dos grupos de la música Mexicana? Se llaman _____ y_____.

16. ¿Cómo se llama una revista o periódico? Se llama _____

17. ¿Para lavar ropa se usa la marca _____?

LA PANADERÍA:

Look for a bakery section or a nearby bakery. Ask these questions directly to an employee if the items are not labeled.

18. ¿Qué tipo de empanadas tienen hoy? _____

19. ¿Cuánto cuestan los churros? Cuesta $_____.

20. ¿De qué colores son los panes dulces que se llaman las conchas? Las conchas son _____ y _____.

EL RESTAURANTE:

Vayan a un restaurante Latino y pidan su comida y bebida en Español.

LESSON 6: CHATTING AT THE RESTAURANT

133 = CIENTO TREINTA Y TRES
THE SUPERMARKET ENGLISH VERSION:

Remember to figure out as much as possible from the Spanish version, before you keep reading this page.

THE FRUITS AND VEGETABLES:

1. What color are nopales=cactus? Red or Green or Brown _____

2. What are some names of different types of chiles? The names are wide chiles, _____ chiles and _____ chiles.

3. How much does a yucca cost? A yucca costs $_____.

4. Plantains are not bananas. How many plantains are there? Many or Few

5. How much does another Latin American vegetable or fruit cost?
   _____ costs $_____ .
   (name of item)   (price)

THE SWEETS:

6. The brand of hot chocolate is Grandma = Abuelita or Mom = Mamá?
   _____

7. What are the flavors of two refreshments, soda pops or juices? For example, the flavors are pineapple, tamarind, _____ and _____.

8. What is the name of a Mexican candy? The name is _____.

9. What are three types of potato chips or crackers/cookies? The types are _____, _____ and _____.

134 = CIENTO TREINTA Y CUATRO

THE TYPICAL FOODS:

10. What are three ingredients in mole sauce? The ingredients are _____ and _____ and _____.

11. What is the symbol on "Bimbo" white bread? (Hint: It looks like the Pillsbury dough boy.) _____

12. How much does prepared tortilla flour or instant corn tortilla dough cost? It costs $_____

13. How many brands of refried beans are there? There are #_____brands.

14. What is the difference between tortillas and tostadas? _____

THE OTHER THINGS:

15. What are the names of two Mexican music groups? The names are _____ and _____.

16. What is the name of a magazine or newspaper? It is called _____.

17. To wash clothes you use the brand name _____.

THE BAKERY:

18. What type of empanadas do they have today? Hint: a pastry pocket with filling. They have _____.

19. How much do your churros cost? They cost $_____.

20. What colors are the sweet breads "the seashells?" The seashells are _____ and _____.

THE RESTAURANT:

Find a restaurant with cuisine from Latin America and celebrate your Spanish achievements. Use the vocabulary in Lesson 6 to help you order your food and drinks in Spanish. ¡Buena suerte! = Good luck!

Recorta = Cut out along the dashed lines

SPANISH CHATBOOK

CERTIFICADO DE RECONOCIMIENTO

Me llamo: _____

La fecha es el _____ de la maestra o el maestro _____

LEARN SPANISH TODAY FOR WORK & PLAY

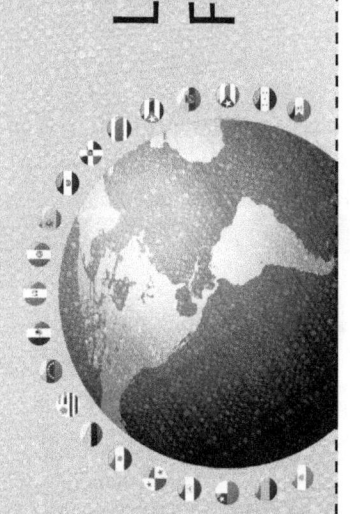

ANSWER KEY

LAS RESPUESTAS = THE ANSWERS

4 = CUATRO

1. banco = bank or bench
2. refrigerador = refrigerator
3. café = coffee, cafe-(a small cafeteria), the color brown
4. teléfono = telephone
5. restaurante = restaurant
6. coliflor = cauliflower

10 = DIEZ

1. C
2. B
3. B
4. A

14 = CATORCE

1. G
2. E
3. B
4. L
5. N
6. M
7. C
8. K
9. D
10. H
11. F
12. I
13. O
14. A
15. J
16. Ñ

LAS RESPUESTAS = THE ANSWERS

20 = VEINTE

CÓMO = how
ESTÁ = are
DÍA = day
NOCHE = night
AYUDAR = to help
ENTIENDE = do you understand
BIEN = Fine
MÁS = more

TARDE = afternoon
MUCHO = much
GUSTO = pleasure
DESPACIO = slow
REPÍTALO = repeat it
POR FAVOR = please or for a favor
USTED = you (formal)
SE LLAMA = You are called (name)

		D	E	S	P	A	C	I	O			
						A	Y	U	D	A	R	S
	D	Í	A								Á	
									E	M		
R	E	P	Í	T	A	L	O		S			E
		M					T		T			D
		U				Á			A			N
T	N	C	Ó	M	O			R	R			E
E	E	H					O		D			I
L	I	O				V			E	N		T
L	B				A					O		N
A				F						C		E
M			R							H		
A		O	T	S	U	G				E		
S		P	U	S	T	E	D					

21 = VEINTIUNO

1. Hello.
2. And you?
3. Good morning.
4. Goodbye!
5. I'm fine.
6. Do you understand?
7. Slow down.
8. Good night.
9. ¿Cómo se llama usted?
10. Repítalo.
11. Buenas tardes.
12. Hasta luego.
13. ¿En qué le puedo ayudar?
14. Mucho gusto.
15. ¿Cómo está usted?
16. Me llamo Julia.

LAS RESPUESTAS = THE ANSWERS

25 = VEINTICINCO

1. Buenos días.
2. ¿Y usted?
3. ¿Cómo está usted?
4. Estoy bien.
5. Mucho gusto.
6. ¿En qué le puedo ayudar?
7. Hasta luego.

28 = VEINTIOCHO

1. C
2. C
3. D
4. A

37 = TREINTA Y SIETE

Interesting things = Cosas interesantes:

1. Cierto.
2. Falso. The eagle was standing on a cactus with a snake in it's mouth.
3. Cierto.

Food = Comida:

1. Falso. A tortilla in Spain would be an omelet with eggs, potatoes, onions, and cheese
2. Cierto.
3. Cierto.

39 = TREINTA Y NUEVE

1. E
2. G
3. M
4. K
5. F
6. D
7. L
8. I
9. B
10. H
11. J
12. C
13. A

LAS RESPUESTAS = THE ANSWERS

41 = CUARENTA Y UNO

1. la hermana = the sister
2. los hermanos = the brothers and sisters
3. la cuenta = the restaurant bill or the account
4. el plato = the plate
5. los tenedores = the forks
6. el cuchillo = the knife
7. la cuchara = the spoon
8. las tazas = the mugs

42 = CUARENTA Y DOS

43 = CUARENTA Y TRES

1. It costs $15.
2. What is your phone number?
3. You're welcome. Have a great day.
4. Sign here.
5. How do you say ___ in Spanish?
6. Where are you from?
7. Soy de los Estados Unidos de América.
8. ¿Cuál es su dirección?
9. ¿Cuánto cuesta?
10. Mi número de teléfono es (967) 555-1384.
11. Espere un momento, por favor.
12. Mi dirección es Calle Principal 246.

LAS RESPUESTAS = THE ANSWERS

45 = CUARENTA Y CINCO

1. mother
2. father
3. son
4. daughter
5. husband
6. wife

49 = CUARENTA Y NUEVE

1. Sí me gusta/No me gusta la comida.
2. Sí me gusta/No me gusta el café con leche.
3. Sí me gusta/No me gusta mi trabajo.
4. Sí me gustan/No me gustan los libros.

55 = CINCUENTA Y CINCO

Interesting things = Cosas interesantes:

1. Cierto.
2. Cierto.
3. Falso. It is freshwater, but there are sharks and tuna fish.

Food = Comida:

1. Cierto.
2. Falso. The fish is actually "cooked" by marinating it in lemon. It is never put in an oven, microwave or cooked on a stove top.
3. Cierto.

LAS RESPUESTAS = THE ANSWERS

56 = CINCUENTA Y SEIS:

1. D
2. C
3. A
4. C

64 = SESENTA Y CUATRO

1. F
2. G
3. A
4. B
5. D
6. E
7. C

65 = SESENTA Y CINCO

Puzzle phrase: ¿Cuántos años tienen sus hijos?

66 = SESENTA Y SEIS

1. I work in a school.
2. Do you have animals?
3. There are ___ people in my family.
4. My daughter's name is Rose.
5. How do you spell (write) that?
6. Best wishes!
7. ¿Dónde trabaja?
8. ¿Cuántos años tienen sus hijos?
9. ¿Cómo se llama su hija?
10. Saludos a su familia.
11. Mis hijos tienen once y trece años.
12. ¿Cuántas personas hay en su familia?

LAS RESPUESTAS = THE ANSWERS

68 = SESENTA Y OCHO

Full Name: (Last(s), First(s) Note: These are plural - explanation on #5 = cinco

Date of Birth: Day   Month   Year   Note: The day comes before the month.

Place of Birth:

Nationality:

Ocupation:

Permanent Address: Street Name   Number   City   State   Zip Code   Country
Note: The number follows the street name.

Marital Status: ☐ Single   ☐ Married   ☐ Divorced   ☐ Widowed

Purpose of Trip: ☐ Pleasure ☐ Convention/Conference   ☐ Business Affairs
  ☐ Study   ☐ Visit Friends and/or Relatives   ☐ Other

Signature   Date

---

70 = SETENTA

1. C
2. A
3. B
4. D
5. C
6. A
7. D
8. B

71 = SETENTA Y UNO

1. the tasty red strawberry = la fresa rica y roja
2. the small black ants = las hormigas negras y pequeñas
3. the way too expensive book = el libro demasiado caro
4. the cheap but good souveniors = los recuerdos baratos pero buenos
5. the silly and young helpers = los ayudantes tontos y divertidos

LAS RESPUESTAS = THE ANSWERS

73 = SETENTA Y TRES

1. H
2. F
3. D
4. E
5. A
6. G
7. C
8. B

75 = SETENTA Y CINCO

1. tengo = I am 40 years old.
2. tiene = Do you have a towel?
3. tenemos = We have a lot of work.
4. tiene = Araceli (Arvaleen) is hungry.
5. tengo = I am cold.
6. tienen = They are not hot.
7. tiene = She is sleepy.
8. tiene = Franco (Frank) is in a hurry.
9. tienen = Melchor (Merle) y Carolina (Carolyn) are not thirsty.
10. tiene = Amelia has to recycle the plastic bottles.

76 = SETENTA Y SEIS

1. quiero = I want to go to a restaurant.
2. quiere = She wants to visit a museum.
3. quiere = Does Ed want to taste a stuffed chile pepper?
4. quiere = Catalina (Sharre Kate) wants to learn a little Spanish.
5. quieren = They want to have better jobs.
6. queremos = We don't want to dance.

77 = SETENTA Y SIETE

1. voy = I am going to make the dinner.
2. va = Eliana goes to Guatemala.
3. van = The customers are going to pay their bills.
4. va = Clara is going to change her clothes.
5. va = Is Natalie going to work tomorrow?
6. vamos = We are going to have the meeting today.

83 = OCHENTA Y TRES

Interesting things = Cosas interesantes:

1. Falso. The Salt Cathedral was carved underground in the salt deposits accessible by tunnels.
2. Cierto.
3. Cierto.

Food = Comida:

1. Cierto.
2. Falso. The first two are true but there is no Pabellón expreso.
3. Cierto.
4.

LAS RESPUESTAS = THE ANSWERS
85 = OCHENTA Y CINCO

										O		
			H	A	B	L	O			C		
									O			C
E		I	N	G	L	É	S		P			O
L						N						N
R					U							P
A	G											E
T	R	O	S	N	E	C	S	A				R
N	B	A	Ñ	O								M
E	C											I
S	I											S
E	A			E	S	P	A	Ñ	O	L		O
R	S											
P			A	I	C	N	E	I	C	A	P	

hablo = I speak

baño = bathroom

con permiso = excuse me

gracias = thank you

ascensor = elevator

español = Spanish

un poco = a little

Inglés = English

paciencia = patience

presentarle = introduce

LAS RESPUESTAS = THE ANSWERS

86 = OCHENTA Y SEIS

1. I'm going to watch television.
2. Excuse me.
3. I would like to introduce you to __.
4. Let's go eat.
5. Thank you for your patience.
6. The elevator is over there.
7. ¿Dónde está el baño?
8. Hablo un poco de español.
9. ¿Cómo llego a ___?
10. ¿Habla inglés?
11. Sígame por aquí.
12. ¿Qué va a hacer?

87 = OCHENTA Y SIETE

"Bingo" game numbers to call out in the following order. Fill out the game board from #87 = ochenta y siete before peeking at these numbers. To help pronounce these in Spanish see the number chart from #24 = veinticuatro. Start with the left column and go down, and then proceed to the second column. Continue until someone yells "Bingo"!

88 = OCHENTA Y OCHO

81-90	801-925	34-40	31-33	101-150
11-15	75-80	302-400	201-250	47-50
21-26	41-46	91-100	712-750	71-74
251-301	401-501	751-800	51-54	1-10
650-711	601-649	151-200	926-1000	16-20
55-60	27-30	61-65	66-70	502-600

89 = OCHENTA Y OCHO

1. 1:00
2. 2:00
3. 3:00
4. 4:00
5. 5:04
6. 6:15
7. 7:30
8. 8:30
9. 8:40
10. 9:45
11. 10:50
12. 11:55

LAS RESPUESTAS = THE ANSWERS

90 = NOVENTA

For the final five, answers will vary. Here are some possible answers.

1. 6:00 A.M.
2. 6:30 A.M.
3. 11:15 A.M.
4. 2:00 P.M.
5. 5:30 P.M.
6. 9:00 P.M

93 = NOVENTA Y TRES

1. D
2. C
3. A
4. D

96 = NOVENTA Y SEIS

1. Ayer fue lunes. = Yesterday was Monday.
2. Ayer fue sábado. = Yesterday was Saturday.
3. Mañana será <u>jueves</u>. = Tomorrow will be Thursday.
4. El mes pasado fue <u>mayo</u>. = The past month was May.
5. El próximo mes será <u>febrero</u>. = Next month would be February.

99 = NOVENTA Y NUEVE

1. F
2. C
3. I
4. K
5. B
6. E
7. L
8. G
9. A
10. H
11. J
12. D

LAS RESPUESTAS = THE ANSWERS

102 = CIENTO DOS

Interesting things = Cosas interesantes:

1. Cierto.
2. Cierto.
3. Falso. Uruguay won the in 1930 and 1950 World Cups.

Food = Comida:

1. Falso. Herbs for Yerba Mate are placed in a gourd, then hot water is poured on the herbs. A "bombilla" metal straw strains the tea as you drink it. When the gourd is empty you usually pass it to the next family member.
2. Cierto
3. Cierto.

106 = CIENTO SEIS

1. estamos
2. está
3. somos
4. es
5. son
6. están

109 = CIENTO NUEVE

Across/Down answers:
- 1. W(ATCHO...) / 2. ALGO MÁS / 3. CUÁNDO / 4. DAY / 5. A(TRILLE) / 6. W(EATHEY) / 7. CUMPLEAÑOS / 8. HUR / 9. HOY / 10. PR / 11. EGUNTAS / 12. NECESITA

LAS RESPUESTAS = THE ANSWERS

110 = CIENTO SEIS

1. Where do you hurt?
2. Today's date is February 13th.
3. Watch out!
4. The appointment is Monday at 9 a.m.
5. What time is it?
6. Do you have questions?
7. ¿Cuál es la fecha de hoy?
8. Me duele la mano.
9. ¿Cuándo es su cumpleaños?
10. Mi cumpleaños es el 17 de junio.
11. ¿Cómo está el clima hoy?
12. ¿Qué día es la cita?
13. ¿Necesita algo más?

112 = CIENTO DOCE

During the summer, my family is going to go to San Juan, Puerto Rico. There are many restaurants, churches, museum, buildings and people. There are almost 1.6 million inhabitants in the Capital area. We will see The St. Phillip Castle (El Morro) and The Yunque Tropical Rainforest. We want to eat fried plantains, beans and chicken with rice and we drank "snow cone" iced drinks. Finally, we are going to relax on the beach.

1. San Juan, Puerto Rico
2. 1.6 million
3. El Morro y El Yunque
4. Tostones, frijoles y arroz

116 = CIENTO DIECISÉIS

1. B
2. D
3. D
4. A
5. B
6. C

117 = CIENTO DIECISIETE

Puzzle phrase: ¿Cuál es su restaurante favorito?

LAS RESPUESTAS = THE ANSWERS

121 = CIENTO VEINTIUNO

Interesting things = Cosas interesantes:

1. Cierto.
2. Cierto.
3. Falso. Equatorial Guinea is located in West Africa.

Food = Comida:

1. Cierto.
2. Falso. Tostones are twice fried plantains that are usually fried in a skillet or deep fat fryer.
3. Cierto.

122 = CIENTO VEINTIDÓS

1. J
2. G
3. F
4. B
5. C
6. A
7. K
8. D
9. N
10. H
11. M
12. L
13. I
14. E

126 = CIENTO VEINTISÉIS

1. cocino, cocina, cocinan
2. trabaja, trabajamos, trabajan
3. como, come, comen
4. asisto, asistimos, asisten

127 = CIENTO VEINTISIETE

1. Yo lavo.
2. Ella llega.
3. Él aprende.
4. Usted lee.
5. Nosotros vivimos.
6. Ellos abren.

LAS RESPUESTAS = THE ANSWERS

128 = CIENTO VEINTIOCHO (Answers will vary.)

1. I like...
2. I don't like...
3. I am...(permanent)
4. I am...(changing)
5. Some day, I am going to...
6. I want to have...
7. My favorite food is...
8. My job is...
9. I need...
10. No one here knows, but in the past I...
11. I would like to meet...(a person)
12. This summer I am going to...
13. I am never able to...
14. A free trip? Perfect! I am going to...with...

130 = CIENTO TREINTA

1. Cheers! Enjoy your meal.
2. What is your favorite food or drink?
3. I am hungry. I am thirsty.
4. I would like to order coffee.
5. Do you like the food?
6. I enjoyed myself very much.
7. La cuenta, por favor.
8. ¿Qué le gustaría?
9. ¿Está todo bien?
10. Bienvenidos. Gracias por venir.
11. Sí, me encanta. Es muy rica.
12. ¿Qué es lo que recomienda?

IGUAZU FALLS = CATARATAS DEL IGUAZÚ IS THE WIDEST IN THE WORLD WITH 270 DISTINCT WATERFALLS. IGUAZU IS LOCATED ON THE BORDER BETWEEN BRAZIL AND ARGENTINA, NEAR PARAGUAY.

GLOSSARY

Spanish = English *(Pronunciation)*

A

¡Adiós! = Goodbye! *(Ah-dee/OHS!)* (Ch. 1)

B

Bienvenidos. = Welcome. *(Bee/ehn-veh-nee-dohs.)* (Ch. 6)

Buen provecho. = Enjoy your meal. *(Bwhen Proh-veh-cho.)* (Ch. 6)

Buenas noches. = Good night. *(Bweh-nahs Noh-chehs.)* (Ch. 1)

Buenas tardes. = Good afternoon. / Good evening. Used from noon until dark. *(Bweh-nahs Tahr-dehs.)* (Ch. 1)

Buenos días. = Good morning. *(Bweh-nohs DEE-ahs.)* (Ch. 1)

C

¿Cómo está el clima hoy? = What is the weather like today? *(KOH-moh Ehs-TAH Ehl Clee-mah Oh/ee?)* (Ch. 5)

¿Cómo está usted? = How are you? *(KOH-moh Ehs-TAH Oos-tehd?)* (Ch. 1)

¿Cómo llego a ___? = How do I get to ___? *(KOH-moh Yeh-goh Ah ___?)* (Ch. 4)

¿Cómo se dice ___ en español? = How do you say ___ in Spanish? *(KOH-moh Seh Dee-seh ___ Ehn Ehs-pah-ñyohl?)* (Ch. 2)

¿Cómo se escribe eso? = How do you spell (write) that? *(KOH-moh Seh Ehs-cree-beh Ehs-oh?)* (Ch. 3)

¿Cómo se llama su hija? = What is your daughter's name? *(KOH-moh Seh Yah-mah Soo Ee-hah?)* (Ch. 3)

¿Cómo se llama usted? ¿Su apellido? = What is your name? Your last name? *(KOH-moh Seh Yah-mah Oos-tehd?) (Soo Ah-peh-yee-doh?)* (Ch. 1)

Con permiso. = Excuse me. *(Kohn Pehr-mee-soh.)* (Ch. 4)

¿Cuándo es su cumpleaños? = When is your birthday? *(Coo/AHN-doh Ehs Soo Koom-pleh-ah-ñyohs?)* (Ch. 5)

¿Cuántas personas hay en su familia? = How many people are in your family? *(Coo/AHN-tahs Pehr-soh-nahs Eye Ehn Soo Fah-mee-lee/ah?)* (Ch. 3)

¿Cuánto cuesta? = How much does it cost? *(Coo/AHN-toh Coo/ehs-tah?)* (Ch. 2)

¿Cuántos años tienen sus hijos? = How old are your children? *(Coo/AHN-tohs Ah-ñyohs Tee-eh-nehn Soos Ee-hohs?)* (Ch. 3)

¿Cuál es la fecha de hoy? = What is the date today? *(Coo/AHL Ehs Lah Feh-cha Deh Oh/ee?)* (Ch. 5)

¿Cuál es su dirección? = What is your address?
(Coo/AHL Ehs Soo Dee-rehk-see/OHN?) (Ch. 2)

¿Cuál es su comida o bebida favorita? = What is your favorite food or drink?
(Coo/AHL Ehs Soo Koh-mee-dah Oh Beh-bee-dah Fah-voh-ree-tah?) (Ch. 6)

¿Cuál es su número de teléfono? = What is your phone number?
(Coo/AHL Ehs Soo NOO-meh-roh Deh Teh-LEH-foh-noh?) (Ch. 2)

Cuesta 15 dólares. = It costs $15. (Coo/ehs-tah Keen-seh DOH-Lah-rehs.) (Ch. 2)

¡Cuidado! = Watch out! (Coo/ee-dah-doh!) OR ¡Ojo! (Oh-ho!) (Ch. 5)

D

¿De dónde es usted? = Where are you from? (Deh DOHN-deh Ehs Oos-tehd?) (Ch. 2)

De nada. = You're welcome. (Deh Nah-dah.) (Ch. 2)

Deseo presentarle a __. = I would like to introduce you to __.
(Deh-seh-oh Preh-sehn-tahr-leh Ah ____.) (Ch. 4)

¿Dónde está el baño? = Where is the bathroom?
(DOHN-deh Ehs-TAH Ehl Bah-ñyoh?) (Ch. 4)

¿Dónde le duele? = Where do you hurt? (DOHN-deh Leh Dweh-leh?) (Ch. 5)

¿Dónde trabaja? = Where do you work? (DOHN-deh Trah-bah-hah?) (Ch. 3)

E

El ascensor está allá. = The elevator is over there.
(Ehl Ah-sehn-sohr Ehs-TAH Ah-YAH.) (Ch. 4)

El ingreso anual = The Annual Income (Ehl Een-greh-soh Ah-noo/ahl)
(Income of Spanish-speaking countries Lessons 2-6)

¿En qué le puedo ayudar? = How may I help you?
(Ehn KEH Leh Pweh-doh Ah-you-dahr?) (Ch. 1)

¿Entiende? = Do you understand? (Ehn-tee/ehn-deh?) (Ch. 1)

Es el 13 de febrero. = Today's date is February 13th.
(Ehs Ehl Treh-seh Deh Feh-breh-roh.) (Ch. 5)

Espere un momento, por favor. = Please wait one moment.
(Ehs-peh-reh Oon Moh-mehn-toh, Pohr Fah-vohr.) (Ch. 2)

¿Está todo bien? = Is everything O.K.? (Ehs-TAH Toh-doh Bee/ehn?) (Ch. 6)

Estoy bien. = I am fine. (Ehs-toy Bee/ehn.) (Ch. 1)

F, G

¡Felicidades! = Best wishes! *(Feh-lee-see-dah-dehs!)* (Ch. 3)

Firme aquí. = Sign here. *(Feer-meh Ah-KEE.)* (Ch. 2)

Gracias por su paciencia. = Thank you for your patience. *(Grah-see/ahs Pohr Soo Pah-see/ehn-see/ah.)* (Ch. 4)

Gracias por venir. = Thank you for coming. *(Grah-see/ahs Pohr Veh-neer.)* (Ch. 6)

H, I, J, K

¿Habla inglés? = Do you speak English? *(Ah-blah Een-GLEHS?)* (Ch. 4)

Hablo un poco de español. = I speak only a little Spanish. *(Ah-bloh Oon Poh-koh Deh Ehs-pah-ñyohl.)* (Ch. 4)

Hasta luego. = See you later. *(Ahs-tah Loo/eh-goh.)* (Ch. 1)

Hay ___ personas en mi familia. = There are ___ people in my family. *(Eye ___ Pehr-soh-nahs Ehn Mee Fah-mee-lee/ah.)* (Ch. 3)

Hola. = Hello. *(Oh-lah.)* (Ch. 1)

L

La comida = The food *(Lah Koh-mee-dah)*
 (Food in Spanish-speaking countries Lessons 2-6)

La cuenta, por favor. = The bill, please. *(Lah Coo/ehn-tah, Pohr Fah-vohr.)* (Ch. 6)

La cita es el lunes a las 9 de la mañana. = The appointment is Monday at 9 a.m. *(Lah See-tah Ehs Ehl Loo-nehs Ah Lahs Noo/eh-veh Deh Lah Mah-ñyah-nah.)* (Ch. 5)

La gente famosa = The famous people *(Lah Hen-teh Fah-moh-sah)*
 (Famous people in Spanish-speaking countries Lessons 2-6)

La moneda nacional = The National currency *(Lah Moh-neh-dah Nah-see/oh-nahl)*
 (Currency of Spanish-speaking countries Lessons 2-6)

La población = The population *(Lah Poh-blah-see/OHN)*
 (Population of Spanish-speaking countries lessons 2-6)

¿Le gusta la comida? = Do you like the food? *(Leh Goose-tah Lah Koh-mee-dah?)* (Ch. 6)

Los lugares para visitar = The places to visit *(Lohs Loo-gah-rehs Pah-rah Vee-see-tahr)*
 (Places to visit in Spanish-speaking countries Lessons 2-6)

M

Más despacio. = Slow down. *(MAHS Dehs-pah-see/oh.)* (Ch. 1)

Me duele la mano. = My hand hurts. *(Meh Dweh-leh Lah Mah-noh.)* (Ch. 5)

Me gustaría pedir un café. = I would like to order coffee.
(Meh Goose-tah-REE/ah Peh-deer Oon Kah-FEH.) (Ch. 6)

Me he divertido mucho. = I enjoyed myself very much.
(Meh Eh Dee-vehr-tee-doh Moo-cho.) (Ch. 6)

Me llamo Julia. = My name is Julie. *(Meh Yah-moh Who-lee/ah.)* (Ch. 1)

Mi cumpleaños es el 17 de junio. = My birthday is June 17th.
(Mee Koom-pleh-ah-ñyohs Ehs Ehl Dee/eh-see-see/eh-teh Deh Who-nee/oh.) (Ch. 5)

Mi dirección es Calle Principal 246. = My address is 246 Main Street.
(Mee Dee-rehk-see/OHN Ehs Kah-yeh Preen-see-pahl Doh-see/ehn-tohs Coo/ah-rent-tah Ee Seh/ace.) (Ch. 2)

Mi hija se llama Rosa. = My daughter's name is Rose.
(Mee Ee-hah Seh Yah-mah Roh-sah.) (Ch. 3)

Mis hijos tienen once y trece años. = My children are 11 and 13 years old.
(Mees Ee-hohs Tee-eh-nehn Ohn-seh Ee Treh-seh Ah-ñyohs.) (Ch. 3)

Mi número de teléfono es (967) 555-1384. = My phone number is (967) 555-1384.
(Mee NOO-meh-roh Deh Teh-LEH-foh-noh Ehs Noo/eh-veh, Seh/ace, See/eh-teh, Seen-koh, Seen-koh, Seen-koh, Treh-seh Oh-chen-tah Ee Coo/ah-troh.) (Ch. 2)

Mucho gusto. = Nice to meet you. *(Moo-cho Goose-toh.)* (Ch. 1)

N, O, P

¿Necesita algo más? = Do you need anything else?
(Neh-seh-see-tah Ahl-goh MAHS?) (Ch. 5)

¡Ojo! *(Oh-ho!)* or ¡Cuidado! = Watch out! *(Coo/ee-dah-doh!)* (Ch. 5)

Q

¿Qué día es la cita? = What day is the appointment?
(KEH DEE-ah Ehs Lah See-tah?) (Ch. 5)

¿Qué es lo que recomienda? = What do you recommend?
(KEH Ehs Loh Keh Reh-koh-mee/ehn-dah?) (Ch. 6)

¿Qué hora es? = What time is it? *(KEH Oh-rah Ehs?)* (Ch. 5)

¿Qué le gustaría? = What would you like? *(KEH Leh Goose-tah-REE/ah?)* (Ch. 6)

Que tenga un buen día. = Have a great day. *(Keh Tehn-gah Oon Bwhen DEE-ah.)* (Ch. 2)

¿Qué va a hacer? = What are you going to do? *(KEH Vah Ah Ah-sehr?)* (Ch. 4)

R, S

Repítalo, por favor. = Repeat that, please. *(Reh-PEE-tah-loh, Pohr Fah-vohr.)* (Ch. 1)

¡Salud! = Cheers! *(Sah-lood!)* (Ch. 6)

Saludos a su familia. = Greetings to your family.
(Sah-loo-dohs Ah Soo Fah-mee-lee/ah.)) (Ch. 3)

Sí, me encanta. Es muy rica. = Yes, I love it. It's delicious.
(SEE, Meh Ehn-kahn-tah. Ehs Moo/ee Ree-kah.) (Ch. 6)

Sígame por aquí. = Follow me over here. *(SEE-gah-meh Pohr Ah-KEE.)* (Ch. 4)

Soy de los Estados Unidos de América. = I am from the U.S.A.
(Soy Deh Lohs Ehs-tah-dohs Oo-knee-dohs Deh Ah-MEH-ree-kah.) (Ch. 2)

T, U

Tengo hambre. Tengo sed. = I am hungry. I am thirsty.
(Tehn-goh Ahm-breh. Tehn-goh Sehd.) (Ch. 6)

¿Tiene animales? = Do you have animals? *(Tee/eh-neh Ah-nee-mah-lehs?)* (Ch. 3)

¿Tiene preguntas? = Do you have questions? *(Tee/eh-neh Preh-goon-tahs?)* (Ch. 5)

Trabajo en una escuela. = I work in a school.
(Trah-bah-hoh Ehn Oo-nah Ehs-kweh-lah.) (Ch. 3)

V, W, X

Vamos a comer. = Let's go eat. *(Vah-mohs Ah Koh-mehr.)* (Ch. 4)

Voy a ver televisión. = I'm going to watch television.
(Voy Ah Vehr Teh-leh-vee-see/OHN.) (Ch. 4)

Y, Z

¿Y usted? = And you? *(Ee Oos-tehd?)* (Ch. 1)

GLOSSARY

English = Spanish *(Pronunciation)*

GLOSSARY: ENGLISH = SPANISH

A

And you? = ¿Y usted? *(Ee Oos-tehd?)* (Ch. 1)

B, C

Best wishes! = ¡Felicidades! *(Feh-lee-see-dah-dehs!)* (Ch. 3)

Cheers! = ¡Salud! *(Sah-lood!)* (Ch. 6)

D

Do you have animals? = ¿Tiene animales? *(Tee/eh-neh Ah-nee-mah-lehs?)* (Ch. 3)

Do you have questions? = ¿Tiene preguntas? *(Tee/eh-neh Preh-goon-tahs?)* (Ch. 5)

Do you like the food? = ¿Le gusta la comida? *(Leh Goose-tah Lah Koh-mee-dah?)* (Ch. 6)

Do you need anything else? = ¿Necesita algo más? *(Neh-seh-see-tah Ahl-goh MAHS?)* (Ch. 5)

Do you speak English? = ¿Habla inglés? *(Ah-blah Een-GLEHS?)* (Ch. 4)

Do you understand? = ¿Entiende? *(Ehn-tee/ehn-deh?)* (Ch. 1)

E

Excuse me. = Con permiso. *(Kohn Pehr-mee-soh.)* (Ch. 4)

Enjoy your meal. = Buen provecho. *(Bwhen Proh-veh-cho.)* (Ch. 6)

F

Follow me over here. = Sígame por aquí. *(SEE-gah-meh Pohr Ah-KEE.)* (Ch. 4)

G

Good afternoon. / Good evening. = Buenas tardes. *(Bweh-nahs Tahr-dehs.)*
    Use Noon-dark (Ch. 1)

Good morning. = Buenos días. *(Bweh-nohs DEE-ahs.)* (Ch. 1)

Good night. = Buenas noches. *(Bweh-nahs Noh-chehs.)* (Ch. 1)

Goodbye! = ¡Adiós! *(Ah-dee/OHS!)* (Ch. 1)

Greetings to your family. = Saludos a su familia.
    (Sah-loo-dohs Ah Soo Fah-mee-lee/ah.) (Ch. 3)

GLOSSARY: ENGLISH = SPANISH

H

Have a great day. = Que tenga un buen día. *(Keh Tehn-gah Oon Bwhen DEE-ah.)* (Ch. 2)

Hello. = Hola. *(Oh-lah.)* (Ch. 1)

How are you? = ¿Cómo está usted? *(KOH-moh Ehs-TAH Oos-tehd?)* (Ch. 1)

How do I get to ___? = ¿Cómo llego a ___? *(KOH-moh Yeh-goh Ah ___?)* (Ch. 4)

How do you say ___ in Spanish? = ¿Cómo se dice ___ en español?
(KOH-moh Seh Dee-seh ___ Ehn Ehs-pah-ñyohl?) (Ch. 2)

How do you spell (write) that? = ¿Cómo se escribe eso?
(KOH-moh Seh Ehs-cree-beh Ehs-oh?) (Ch. 3)

How may I help you? = ¿En qué le puedo ayudar?
(Ehn KEH Leh Pweh-doh Ah- you-dahr?) (Ch. 1)

How many people are in your family? = ¿Cuántas personas hay en su familia?
(Coo/AHN-tahs Pehr-soh-nahs Eye Ehn Soo Fah-mee-lee/ah?) (Ch. 3)

How much does it cost? = ¿Cuánto cuesta? *(Coo/AHN-toh Coo/ehs-tah?)* (Ch. 2)

How old are your children? = ¿Cuántos años tienen sus hijos?
(Coo/AHN-tohs Ah-ñyohs Tee-eh-nehn Soos Ee-hohs?) (Ch. 3)

I, J, K

I am hungry. I am thirsty. = Tengo hambre. Tengo sed.
(Tehn-goh Ahm-breh. Tehn-goh Sehd.) (Ch. 6)

I am fine. = Estoy bien. *(Ehs-toy Bee/ehn.)* (Ch. 1)

I am from the U.S.A. = Soy de los Estados Unidos de América.
(Soy Deh Lohs Ehs-tah-dohs Oo-knee-dohs Deh Ah-MEH-ree-kah.) (Ch. 2)

I enjoyed myself very much. = Me he divertido mucho. =
(Meh Eh Dee-vehr-tee-doh Moo-cho.) (Ch. 6)

I speak only a little Spanish. = Hablo un poco de español.
(Ah-bloh Oon Poh-koh Deh Ehs-pah-ñyohl.) (Ch. 4)

I work in a school. = Trabajo en una escuela.
(Trah-bah-hoh Ehn Oo-nah Ehs-kweh-lah.) (Ch. 3)

I would like to introduce you to ___. = Deseo presentarle a ___.
(Deh-seh-oh Preh-sehn-tahr-leh Ah ___.) (Ch. 4)

I would like to order coffee. = Me gustaría pedir un café.
(Meh Goose-tah-REE/ah Peh-deer Oon Kah-FEH.) (Ch. 6)

I'm going to watch television. = Voy a ver televisión.
(Voy Ah Vehr Teh-leh-vee-see/OHN.) (Ch. 4)

Is everything O.K.? = ¿Está todo bien? *(Ehs-TAH Toh-doh Bee/ehn?)* (Ch. 6)

It costs $15. = Cuesta 15 dólares. *(Coo/ehs-tah Keen-seh DOH-Lah-rehs.)* (Ch. 2)

L

Let's go eat. = Vamos a comer. *(Vah-mohs Ah Koh-mehr.)* (Ch. 4)

M

My address is 246 Main Street. = Mi dirección es Calle Principal 246.
(Mee Dee-rehk-see/OHN Ehs Kah-yeh Preen-see-pahl Doh-see/ehn-tohs Coo/ah-rent-tah Ee Seh/ace.) (Ch. 2)

My birthday is June 17th. = Mi cumpleaños es el 17 de junio.
(Mee Koom-pleh-ah-ñyohs Ehs Ehl Dee/eh-see-see/eh-teh Deh Who-nee/oh.) (Ch. 5)

My children are 11 and 13 years old. = Mis hijos tienen once y trece años.
(Mees Ee-hohs Tee-eh-nehn Ohn-seh Ee Treh-seh Ah-ñyohs.) (Ch. 3)

My daughter's name is Rose. = Mi hija se llama Rosa.
(Mee Ee-hah Seh Yah-mah Roh-sah.) (Ch. 3)

My hand hurts. = Me duele la mano. *(Meh Dweh-leh Lah Mah-noh.)* (Ch. 5)

My name is Julie. = Me llamo Julia. *(Meh Yah-moh Who-lee/ah.)* (Ch. 1)

My phone number is (967) 555-1384. = Mi número de teléfono es (967) 555-1384.
(Mee NOO-meh-roh Deh Teh-LEH-foh-noh Ehs Noo/eh-veh, Seh/ace, See/eh-teh, Seen-koh, Seen-koh, Seen-koh, Treh-seh Oh-chen-tah Ee Coo/ah-troh.) (Ch. 2)

N, O

Nice to meet you. = Mucho gusto. *(Moo-cho Goose-toh.)* (Ch. 1)

P, Q

Please wait one moment. = Espere un momento, por favor.
(Ehs-peh-reh Oon Moh-mehn-toh, Pohr Fah-vohr.) (Ch. 2)

R

Repeat that, please. = Repítalo, por favor. *(Reh-PEE-tah-loh, Pohr Fah-vohr.)* (Ch. 1)

S

See you later. = Hasta luego. *(Ahs-tah Loo/eh-goh.)* (Ch. 1)

Sign here. = Firme aquí. *(Feer-meh Ah-KEE.)* (Ch. 2)

Slow down. = Más despacio. *(MAHS Dehs-pah-see/oh.)* (Ch. 1)

T, U, V

Thank you for coming. = Gracias por venir. *(Grah-see/ahs Pohr Veh-neer.)* (Ch. 6)

Thank you for your patience. = Gracias por su paciencia.
(Grah-see/ahs Pohr Soo Pah-see/ehn-see/ah.) (Ch. 4)

The Annual Income = El ingreso anual *(Ehl Een-greh-soh Ah-noo/ahl)*
(Income of Spanish-speaking countries Lessons 2-6)

The bill, please. = La cuenta, por favor. *(Lah Coo/ehn-tah, Pohr Fah-vohr.)* (Ch. 6)

The elevator is over there. = El ascensor está allá.
(Ehl Ah-sehn-sohr Ehs-TAH Ah-YAH.) (Ch. 4)

The famous people = La gente famosa *(Lah Hen-teh Fah-moh-sah)*
(Famous people in Spanish-speaking countries Lessons 2-6)

The food = La comida *(Lah Koh-mee-dah)* (In Spanish-speaking countries Lessons 2-6)

The National currency = La moneda nacional *(Lah Moh-neh-dah Nah-see/oh-nahl)*
(The currency of Spanish-speaking countries Lessons 2-6)

The places to visit = Los lugares para visitar *(Lohs Loo-gah-rehs Pah-rah Vee-see-tahr)*
(The places to visit in Spanish-speaking countries Lessons 2-6)

The population = La población *(Lah Poh-blah-see/OHN)*
(The population of Spanish-speaking countries Lessons 2-6)

There are ___ people in my family. = Hay ___ personas en mi familia.
(Eye ___ Pehr-soh-nahs Ehn Mee Fah-mee-lee/ah.) (Ch. 3)

The appointment is Monday at 9 a.m. = La cita es el lunes a las 9 de la mañana.
(Lah See-tah Ehs Ehl Loo-nehs Ah Lahs Noo/eh-veh Deh Lah Mah-ñyah-nah.) (Ch. 5)

Today's date is February 13th. = Es el 13 de febrero.
(Ehs Ehl Treh-seh Deh Feh-breh-roh.) (Ch. 5)

W, X

Watch out! = ¡Cuidado! *(Coo/ee-dah-doh!)* Or ¡Ojo! *(Oh-ho!)* (Ch. 5)

Welcome. = Bienvenidos. *(Bee/ehn-veh-nee-dohs.)* (Ch. 6)

What are you going to do? = ¿Qué va a hacer? *(KEH Vah Ah Ah-sehr?)* (Ch. 4)

What day is the appointment? = ¿Qué día es la cita?
(KEH DEE-ah Ehs Lah See-tah?) (Ch. 5)

What do you recommend? = ¿Qué es lo que recomienda?
(KEH Ehs Loh Keh Reh-koh-mee/ehn-dah?) (Ch. 6)

What is the date today? = ¿Cuál es la fecha de hoy?
(Coo/AHL Ehs Lah Feh-cha Deh Oh/ee?) (Ch. 5)

What is the weather like today? = ¿Cómo está el clima hoy?
(KOH-moh Ehs-TAH Ehl Clee-mah Oh/ee?) (Ch. 5)

What is your address? = ¿Cuál es su dirección?
(Coo/AHL Ehs Soo Dee-rehk-see/OHN?) (Ch. 2)

What is your daughter's name? = ¿Cómo se llama su hija?
(KOH-moh Seh Yah-mah Soo Ee-hah?) (Ch. 3)

What is your favorite food or drink? = ¿Cuál es su comida o bebida favorita?
(Coo/AHL Ehs Soo Koh-mee-dah Oh Beh-bee-dah Fah-voh-ree-tah?) (Ch. 6)

What is your name? Your last name? = ¿Cómo se llama usted? ¿Su apellido?
(KOH-moh Seh Yah-mah Oos-tehd?) (Soo Ah-peh-yee-doh?) (Ch. 1)

What is your phone number? = ¿Cuál es su número de teléfono?
(Coo/AHL Ehs Soo NOO-meh-roh Deh Teh-LEH-foh-noh?) (Ch. 2)

What time is it? = ¿Qué hora es? *(KEH Oh-rah Ehs?)* (Ch. 5)

What would you like? = ¿Qué le gustaría? *(KEH Leh Goose-tah-REE/ah?)* (Ch. 6)

When is your birthday? = ¿Cuándo es su cumpleaños?
(Coo/AHN-doh Ehs Soo Koom-pleh-ah-ñyohs?) (Ch. 5)

Where are you from? = ¿De dónde es usted? *(Deh DOHN-deh Ehs Oos-tehd?)* (Ch. 2)

Where do you work? = ¿Dónde trabaja? *(DOHN-deh Trah-bah-hah?)* (Ch. 3)

Where do you hurt? = ¿Dónde le duele? *(DOHN-deh Leh Dweh-leh?)* (Ch. 5)

Where is the bathroom? = ¿Dónde está el baño?
(DOHN-deh Ehs-TAH Ehl Bah-ñyoh?) (Ch. 4)

Y, Z

Yes, I love it. It's delicious. = Sí, me encanta. Es muy rica.
(SEE, Meh Ehn-kahn-tah. Ehs Moo/ee Ree-kah.) (Ch. 6)

You're welcome. = De nada. *(Deh Nah-dah.)* (Ch. 2)

BONUS ITEMS

Here is an extra final project as described in Lesson 3. For more information and other final project ideas see #61 = sesenta y uno.

The travel agency = La agencia de viaje: You are a travel agent advertising your country so people will want to come to visit. You must make a brochure, poster or computer presentation about your country. Include a map of your country, pictures or drawings, newspaper clippings, and anything else representing the country. You will need to include at least at least 12 sentences IN SPANISH describing the following:

1. The name of the country and the capital. Example: Mi país se llama _____. y la capital se llama_____.

2. The name of the money and how much one U.S. dollar equals. The exchange rate changes daily and can be found on the Internet.

3. The population and/or size of the country

4. What three things could a tourist do or see in your country?

5. What could a tourist try eating or what products could they buy as souvenirs?

6. What music, dance, typical sport, or famous artwork could they enjoy?

7. What is the government like? Any historical sites?

8. Who are some famous people from your country and why are they famous?

9. Describe the flag: Example: La bandera tiene los colores _____.) (Include an example of a flag)

10. What are some holidays your country celebrates?

11. What animals are native to your country?

12. What is the weather like in December in your country?

The recipes = Las recetas:

1. **Tortilla de patatas (Spain):** A Tortilla de patatas is made with 2 onions, 4 potatoes and 6 eggs. Heat olive oil in a deep fat fryer. This can also be done in a skillet. Heat enough olive oil to cover the potatoes; this may be a cup or more of oil. Cut the potatoes and onions into small (1/2 inch) slices and fry them until brown. Lightly salt them to taste. In a separate bowl, stir the eggs a few times without beating them. Add the potatoes/onions to the eggs. Heat 1 tablespoon of olive oil in a skillet and add the egg/potato/onions mixture. Cook on medium heat for about 10 minutes. Top the skillet with a plate and flip it over. Heat 1 tablespoon of olive oil in the skillet and slide the "tortilla de patatas" back into the pan. Heat for about 5–10 minutes. Eat hot or cold. In Spain they use long baguette bread and put the "tortilla de patatas" inside as a sandwich. You will find one triangle piece of tortilla de patatas as a typical tapas dish. (See #36 = treinta y seis y #37 = treinta y siete for an explanation of tapas.)

2. **Tortillas/Pupusas/Arepas (Latin America):** It is easy to make your own tortillas. Buy "harina preparada para las tortillas" (tortilla flour). Take either the corn or white tortilla flour and then add the water and salt according to the package. Roll a ball and then shape them with a tortilla press. If you don't have a tortilla press, push a plate down onto the dough to cut a circle or press the tortilla into a circle with your hands. Hint: You may want to use wax paper on each side of the dough ball to prevent it from sticking to the tortilla press. Finally, cook the tortilla on an electric skillet or pancake griddle for just a few minutes on each side. Finally, sprinkle them with cinnamon and sugar or top with salsa and cheese. To make pupusas or arepas follow the same steps, but make the dough thicker. ¡Qué rico! = How tasty!

3. **Gallo Pinto (Costa Rica):** In Nicaragua and Honduras, Gallo Pinto is usually made with red beans, whereas in Costa Rica, it is made with black beans. To make Gallo Pinto, heat 1 tablespoon of olive oil in a skillet. Sauté 1 chopped white onion and 2 cloves of garlic. Stir in one can of cooked black beans. (Do not drain.) Add 2 cups of cooked white rice and 1 teaspoon of Worcestershire sauce to the bean mix, and simmer for 5–10 minutes. Add a dash or two of crushed red pepper to taste. Chop some fresh cilantro and add that to the Gallo Pinto, but be careful because a small amount is very flavorful. Heat the mixture thoroughly and serve for breakfast with scrambled eggs.

4. **CUBAN SANDWICHES (CUBA):** Slice one loaf of Cuban, Italian, or French bread into 4 parts. Split each part in half so that it is ready to fill. Spread mayonnaise or mustard on the bottom part of the bread. Stack the bread with sliced ham, roast pork, thin dill pickle slices and slices of Swiss cheese. Now add the top half of the bread. Brush with olive oil or butter. Put a heavy skillet on top of the sandwiches before grilling or baking in the oven. This will press them flat. Use a sandwich press for the same results. Bake them in the oven at 350 degrees until the cheese is melted.

5. **MANGO GELATIN (CENTRAL AMERICA):** Gelatin or flan or other kinds of pudding mixes may be found in a local grocery store or on the Internet. Some of the flavors are tembleque (a coconut dish), cajeta (like caramel), chocolate flan, walnut, sherry, piña (pineapple), peach and many more.

6. **HORCHATA (MÉXICO):** Horchata, guanabana, tamarindo, sandía (watermelon), jamaica (hibiscus flower), mango and many other flavors of powdered drink mixes may be purchased from the grocery store. Aguas Frescas come in many varieties. Simply mix with water to make a single serving or a pitcher full.

7. **CHICHA/MAZAMORRA (PERÚ):** It is easy to make a purple corn pudding called Mazamorra and a purple corn drink called Chicha Morada. Both of these packaged mixes may be ordered from various Web sites. Serve them with Inca Kola. It's a yellow carbonated soft drink tasting like bubble gum.

8. **QUESADILLAS (MÉXICO):** Quesadillas are easy to make with a quesadilla maker or by folding one tortilla in half and cooking it on a sandwich-type grill. With a quesadilla maker, use two burrito-sized flour tortilla shells and fill them with your favorite meats and cheeses. Add salsa, black beans, corn and other spices. For a twist, make sweet, dessert quesadillas by adding cooked apples or slices of banana, cinnamon, and brown sugar to the plain tortillas and then cooking them. Serve with vanilla ice cream or whipped cream.

9. **TOSTADAS (MÉXICO):** To make tostadas buy a package of tostada shells or fry your own. Spread with refried beans, then add chopped tomatoes and shredded lettuce. Top with Oaxacan or cheddar cheese, salsa and sliced avocados. Use any additional toppings as desired.

10. **Arroz con leche (Spain/Latin America):** To make this rice pudding, boil 4 cups of water with cinnamon. Add 2 cups of minute rice and cover for 5 minutes. Follow the package directions for other types of rice. Combine the rice with one can of sweetened condensed milk, one can of evaporated milk, a splash of vanilla, a dash of nutmeg and raisins. Add more rice to make a thicker pudding. Refrigerate for 1 hour and sprinkle cinnamon on top before serving.

11. **Sopapillas (México):** Mix together 1 teaspoon of salt, 2 teaspoons baking powder and 4 cups flour. Cut in 4 tablespoons of shortening. Measure 1 1/2 cups warm water and add to the dry ingredients. Mix the dough until it is smooth. Cover and let the dough rest for 20 minutes. Next, sprinkle flour onto a board and roll the dough until it is about 1/4 inch thick. Cut the dough into squares of about 3 inches. Add 2 quarts oil into a deep-fat fryer and heat to 375 degrees F. Use a candy thermometer to check that the oil is exactly 375 degrees so the sopapillas will puff up. Fry until golden brown, flipping them over halfway through. Put them on a plate with paper towels. Sprinkle with cinnamon and sugar. Serve them warm. Remember to reheat the oil to 375 between batches. This recipe makes about 2 dozen.

12. **Chicle = Chewing gum (Latin America):** Make your own chewing gum with a kit benefiting the chicleros in the rainforest. Chicleros are people who collect the sap from the chicle (gum) tree. Kits include the sap to melt and all of the ingredients. Kits to make your own gum can be found online.

13. **Chocolate (South America):** Chocolate comes from the cocoa bean pod, which may be found in the rainforests of Central and South America. Many companies sell authentic Latin American chocolates on the Internet and in Hispanic grocery stores. Make your own chocolate lollipops by melting chocolate chips and pouring them into any candy mold. Add lollipop sticks and freeze for about 10 minute. Kits to make your own chocolate candies from scratch can be found online.

14. **Chocolate caliente = Hot chocolate (México):** There are many different brands of Mexican Hot chocolate, such as "Ibarra" and "Abuelita." Blend the chocolate/cinnamon bark in the blender with hot milk to make a delicious drink in cold weather. Be sure to hold the top on the blender so the mixture doesn't fly out. Hot chocolate is even served for breakfast in Oaxaca, México.

15. **Dulces = Candies (Latin America):** One idea is to sample different candies from México, Spain and other countries. Latin Americans have been using candies and small toys to fill up piñatas for many years. Piñatas may have originated in Europe with a painted clay pot filled with candies and coins. A star-shaped piñata probably represented the Star of Bethlehem at Christmas time and is still used in the December Posadas celebrations. Now there are many designs from animals to cartoon characters. Find Web sites showing different styles of piñatas. To make your own piñata, start with an inflated balloon. Use newspaper dipped into liquid starch to cover the balloon. After it dries for a few days, decorate the piñata with tissue paper. Paint the tissue paper with watered down Elmer's glue to get it to stick to the piñata. Let this dry and then fill it with candy. In Cuba they attach strings to the piñata and instead of using a bat, everyone grabs a string and pulls the piñata apart.

16. **Pan Dulce = Sweet bread (Latin America):** "Pan Dulce" sweet breads are available at many bakeries or make your own. Check for Pan de los Muertos (The Bread of the Dead) the first few days of November. Look for the 3 Kings cakes (January 6) and Mardi Gras cakes (before Ash Wednesday). These cakes have a baby hidden inside and whoever finds the baby has to have the next fiesta. Sometimes they hide a coin inside the cake. Be careful while eating this one.

17. **Chicharrones (México):** Chicharrones are fried pork rinds. Buy them raw and they look like pasta wagon wheels. After you fry them, they puff up and may be dipped into salsa or sprinkled with cinnamon and sugar. It may be easier to buy them pre-cooked in bags usually located in the chip aisle at the grocery store.

18. **Tostones (Puerto Rico):** Tostones are fried plantains. The plantain looks like a huge banana, but it is really more like a potato so don't eat it raw. Heat 1/2 cup of oil in a skillet. Cut the plantain into circle slices. Fry the slices and then remove them from the skillet. Flatten them by smashing them with a plate or the bottom of a glass or use a "tostonera" from Puerto Rico. Dip the plantains in water, and then fry them again in the hot oil. Salt to taste and eat these while warm. Pre-packaged banana chips can be found in some grocery stores.

19. **QUESO FUNDIDO = CHEESE DIP (MÉXICO):** Cheese dip can be made by melting a processed block cheese and salsa together. Or use a can of tomatoes and add cooked ground beef or chorizo. For a more authentic queso dip use Oaxacan cheese or any other fresh Mexican cheese that melts really well. Serve with chips.

20. **CHURROS (SPAIN):** Churros resemble long cinnamon sugar breadsticks. The dough may be made by combining 2 cups biscuit mix and 1 and 3/4 cups hot water. Stir for a few minutes. Roll the dough into long tubes or squeeze through a pastry bag. Fry 2 at a time in a deep fat fryer and then roll in a mixture of cinnamon and sugar. Eat warm. Other authentic churro recipes can be found on the internet.

21. **FLAN (LATIN AMERICA):** To make flan, put 1 cup of sugar in a saucepan and stir constantly on medium/low heat until liquid. Quickly pour the "caramel" to the bottom of a 10-inch pie plate or flan mold. In a separate bowl, stir 3 large eggs lightly. Add 1 can of evaporated milk, 1 can of sweetened condensed milk and 1 tablespoon of vanilla to the eggs. Gently stir to mix, do not beat. Pour into the pie plate or mold. Use a double boiler or put about 1 inch of boiling water in a larger pan and put the pie plate inside. This is called a Baño María = Maria's bath. Bake at 325 degrees for approximately 45 minutes. Refrigerate overnight or at least 4 hours and then flip over onto a serving dish allowing the caramel to drizzle across the top. It may be easier to buy a package of flan mix in the pudding aisle at the grocery store and just add milk.

22. **ENCHILADAS (MÉXICO):** To make enchiladas, start by browning one pound of hamburger. Add 3 ounces of cream cheese, 1 cup of salsa, 1/2 tablespoon of cumin, and 1 cup of shredded fiesta cheese to the hamburger. Grease a 9x13 pan. Put 3 spoonfuls of the hamburger mixture in one burrito-size tortilla and roll it up. About 6 burritos will fit in the pan. Then cover with 1 jar of enchilada sauce. Top with the remaining 1 cup of fiesta cheese and bake uncovered at 350 degrees F for 40 minutes.

23. **SALSA (LATIN AMERICA):** In a blender or food processor, combine 2 chopped green onions and 1 diced clove of garlic. Add cilantro, crushed red pepper and salt to taste. Add 2 1/2 cups of tomatoes fresh from the garden. Blend for a few seconds and serve with blue corn tortilla chips

24. **OTHER RECIPES:** You can find many other recipes in cookbooks or online. **¡BUEN PROVECHO! = ENJOY YOUR MEAL!**

SUBJECT INDEX

A

Accent marks, Introduction to, 7
Acquisition language, 27, 38
Activity, phrases, 69
Adjectives,
    Introduction to, 71
Advice, travel, 123
AEIOU/vowels, 1, 3
Age, 50-51, 75
Aid, First, Health, list of vocabulary, 97-98
Alphabet, 58-59
Answer key, 137-152
Americas
    Central, 52, 53-55, 113
    North 18-19, 29, 32, 36-38, 52, 91
    South, 71, 79, 81-83, 100-102
    Speaking Spanish throughout, 79
Application for customs, 68
-ar verb conjugation, Present tense, 124-127
Argentina, 71, 79, 83, 101-102
Around the world game, 84
Audio track list, 22
Aztecs 32, 36, 96

B

Beginning of the meal phrases, restaurants, 114
Best wishes, phrases, 60
Bingo, game directions, 62-63, 87, 128, 147
Body parts, 98
Bolivia, 81, 100, 102
Business,
    Customers,
        Greeting, 8-9
        Introductions, 3, 8
    Directions, giving and receiving, 72
    Employees,
        Latino, supervision, 52
        Personal descriptions, 50-51
        Tardiness, 91
    Greetings, 8-9
    Introductions, 3, 8
    Latin American schedules, 113
    Personal descriptions, 50-51

C

Calendar,
    Aztec, 32, 36
    Days of the week, 93
    Phrases, 95
    Weather, 94
Categorizing, Hispanics and Latinos, 18-19
CD/Audio track list, 22
Central American countries,
    Costa Rica, 52, 54-55, 113
    El Salvador, 52, 53, 55
    Guatemala, 18, 52, 53, 55
    Honduras, 52, 53, 55
    Nicaragua, 52, 53, 55
    Panamá, 52, 54-55
Certificate of completion, 135
Chicanos, 18
Chile, 81, 100, 102
Choosing, Spanish name, Intro, 3, 9
Cognates, 4
Colombia, 81-83
Colors, Introduction to, 71
Communication, styles, 118
Connect with others, phrases, 27
Connections, language phrases, 78
Conquistadors, 79
Consonants, 2
Contact, Initial phrases, 26
Continue learning in the future, 10 ideas, 129
Conversation starters, 128
Conversations, role plays, 16, 32-33, 57, 80, 103, 115
Costa Rica, 101-102, 173, 182, 196
Countries,
    Central America,
        Costa Rica, 52, 54-55, 113
        El Salvador, 52, 53, 55
        Guatemala, 18, 52, 53, 55
        Honduras, 52, 53, 55
        Nicaragua, 52, 53, 55
        Panamá, 52, 54-55
    Equatorial Guinea, 121-122
    Island nations,
        Cuba, 121-122
        Dominican Republic, 91, 121-122

SUBJECT INDEX

Puerto Rico, 91, 112, 121-122, 150
México, 18-19, 29, 32, 36-38, 52, 91
South America,
    Argentina, 71, 79, 81, 101-102
    Bolivia, 81, 100, 102
    Chile, 81, 100, 102
    Colombia, 81-83
    Ecuador, 81-83
    Paraguay, 81, 101-102
    Perú, 81, 100, 102
    Uruguay, 81, 101-102
    Venezuela, 81-83
Spain, 11, 18-19, 36-38, 79, 91, 113
Crossword puzzle, 42, 109
Cuba, 121-122
Customers, Greetings, 8

D

Daily routine, 89
Days of the week, 93, 96
Descriptions,
    Age, 50-51, 75
    Body parts, 98
    Colors, Introduction of, 71
    Days of the week, 93, 96
    Dislikes, 49-51
    Family,
        Descriptions, 50-51
        Hispanic, 52
        Members, 45-46
        Presentation, 67
        Project, 50-51
        Tree, 5
    Job, 50-51
    Likes, 49-51
Desktop phrase guide, 23
Differences, gender, 52
Directions, giving and receiving, 72
Dislikes, likes,
    Introduction to, 49-51
Diversity in the Spanish language, 38
Dominican Republic, 91, 121-122
During the meal phrases, restaurants, 119

E

Eating times, 113
Ecuador, 81-83
El Salvador, 52, 53, 55
Employees,
    Latino, supervision, 52
English vs. Spanish,

Acquisition of language, 27, 38
    Glossary of phrases, 153-164
Equatorial Guinea, 121-122
-er verb conjugation, Present tense 124-127
Establish rapport, phrases, 48
Estar vs. Ser, the verb to be, Present tense 104-106
Etiquette,
    Greetings, 3, 8-9   Helpful introductory phrases 13
    Restaurant, 114, 119
    Tardiness, 91
    Tú vs. Usted, 11
    Travel, 123
Event scheduling phrases, 95
Exam, translation exercise, 21, 43, 66, 89, 110, 130
Expressing likes and dislikes, 49-51

F

Facts,
    Spanish-speaking countries, 36, 53, 54, 82, 100, 101, 120
    Historical, 79
    Interesting 37, 55, 83, 102, 121
Family,
    Descriptions, 50-51
    Hispanic, 52
    Members, 45-46
    Phrases, 56
    Presentation, 67
    Project, 50-51
    Tree, 5
Famous people, 19, 36, 53, 54, 82, 100, 101, 120
Field trip, 131-134

Fiesta,
    For the class, 107, 111, 129
    In Latin America, 91
Final project
    Ideas, 61, 165
    Presentations 111
First Aid, phrases, 97
Flashcards, cut out after game page in each lesson
Fluency, language, 38
Food,
    Grocery store scavenger hunt, 131-134
    Information, Countries 36, 53, 54, 82, 100, 101, 120
    Menu, 113
    Phrases, 114, 119
    Trivia about countries, 37, 55, 83, 102, 121
Future ideas- to continue learning, 129

SUBJECT INDEX

G

Games,
    Around the world, 84
    Bingo, 62-63, 87, 128, 147
    Más o Menos, 30
    Tic-Tac-Toe, 15, 108
    Toma Todo, 40, 108
    True/False, 107
Gender differences, 52
Giving and receiving directions, 72
Glossary of phrases, 153-164
Goals, survey needs, Intro
Goodbye phrases, 8
Guatemala, 18, 52, 53, 55
Grammar,
    Adjectives, 71
    English vs. Spanish, 27, 38
    Tú vs. Usted, 11
    Usted vs. Tú, 11
    Verbs, *see also*
Greetings, introduction to, 8-9
Gringos, 18
Grocery store scavenger hunt, 131-134
Gustar, likes, dislikes, Introduction to, 49-51

H

Health words,
    Medical phrases, 97
Helpful introductory phrases, 13
Hispanic,
    Americans, 19
    Families, 52, 91
    Latino, categorizing, 18-19
    Restaurant customer service, 114,119
Historical
    Perspectives, 79
    Figures, 19, 36, 53, 54, 82, 100, 101, 120
History of Spanish-speaking countries, 35, 79
Holidays, 91
Honduras, 52, 53, 55
Human resources, phrases, 26, 27, 95
How to learn to read Spanish in five minutes, 1-2

I

Ideas to continue learning in the future, 129
Important phrases, 8, 13, 26, 27, 31, 48, 56, 60, 69, 72, 78, 95, 97, 114, 119
Incas, 96, 100, 102
Information, personal, 26, 27, 48, 56
Initial contact phrases, 26

Introductions, Intro, 3, 8-9
Introductory phrases, helpful, 13
Ir, 77
-ir verb conjugation,
    Present tense, 124-127
Islands, 91, 112, 121-122, 150

J, K, L

Job, descriptions, 50-51
Language
    Acquisition, English vs. Spanish, 27, 38
    Connection phrases, 78
    Fluency, 38
Latin American schedules, 113
Latino and Hispanic categorizing, 18-19
Latino employees' supervision, 52
Leisure activity phrases, 69
Lesson plans,
    Continuing education ideas, 129
    Family project, 50-51
    Field trip, 131-134
    Fiesta,
        For the class, 129
        In Latin America, 91
    Grocery store scavenger hunt, 129
    Presentations,
        Family, 67
        Final, 61, 111,165
Likes/dislikes,
    Introduction to, 49-51
Locating Central American countries, 52

M

Machismo, 52
Make connections, phrases, 27
Manager phrases, 26, 27, 95
Mañana, 91, 96
Map, of Spanish Speaking countries, 24
Matching activities, 14, 39, 64, 73, 99, 122
Mayas, 47, 96
Meal phrases, 114, 119
Medical phrases, 97
Members of the family, 45-46
Menu, 113
Mexican, 18, 36-37, 91, 131-134
Mexican-Americans, 18
México, 18-19, 29, 32, 36-38, 52, 91
Months of the year, 92-93, 96
Multiple choice exercises, 10, 28, 56, 70, 93, 116

N

Names,
    Choosing, Spanish name list, Intro
    Introductions, last name 3, 5-6
    Famous people, 19, 36, 53, 54, 82, 100, 101, 120
    Name tag, Intro, 11
Nicaragua, 52, 53, 55
Numbers,
    Introduction to, chart, 24
    Mayan system, 47

O, P

Order form, 176
Panamá, 52, 54-55
Paraguay, 81, 101-102
People,
    Connections, phrases, 27
    Famous 19 36, 53, 54, 82, 100, 101, 120
Personal descriptions, 26, 27, 48, 50-51, 56
Personal questions, 26, 27, 48, 56
Perú, 81, 100, 102
Phrases, important, 8, 13, 26, 27, 31, 48, 56, 60, 69, 72, 78, 95, 97, 114, 119
Phrases, introductory, helpful, 13
Present tense verbs,
    -ar Introduction to, regular 124-127
    -er Introduction to, regular 124-127
    -ir, Introduction to, regular 124-127
Presentations,
    Family, 50-51, 67
    Final project, 61, 111, 165
Pricing, phrases, 31
Professions/ jobs,
    Basic descriptions, 50-51
Projects, final 61, 165
Pronouns, 49, 74
Pronunciations of vowels and consonants, 1-2
Puerto Rico, 91, 112, 121-122, 150
Puzzle,
    Crossword, 42, 109
    Secret phrase, 65, 117
    Word search, 20, 79

Q, R

Querer, 76
Question, see also phrases
    Personal, 48
    Words, 34

Rapport building phrases, 48
Receiving directions, phrases 72
Recipes, 166-170
Reflexive verbs,
    Introduction to, 89
Regular verbs,
    -ar present tense, 124-127
    -er present tense, 124-127
    -ir present tense, 124-127
Restaurant
    Etiquette and lingo, 113, 114, 119
    Customer service phrases, 114, 119
Role plays, conversations, 16, 32-33, 57, 80, 103, 115
Roll an R, tongue muscle, 2

S

Scavenger hunt, 131-134
Schedules,
    Latin America, 113
    Phrases, 95
Secret phrase puzzle, 65, 117
Ser vs. estar, the verb to be, 104-106
Servers to Hispanic customers, 113, 114, 119
Shopping phrases, 31
South America,
    Argentina, 71, 79, 81, 101-102
    Bolivia, 81, 100, 102
    Chile, 81, 100, 102
    Colombia, 81-83
    Ecuador, 81-83
    Paraguay, 81, 101-102
    Perú, 81, 100, 102
    Uruguay, 81, 101-102
    Venezuela, 81-83
Spain, 11, 18-19, 36-38, 79, 91, 113
Spaniards, 18, 36-38
Spanish language,
    Accent marks, 7
    Adjectives, 71
    AEIOU, 1, 3
    Alphabet, 58-59
    American, speaking Spanish, 18-19
    Diversity, 38
    English vs. Spanish, 27, 38
    Glossary, 153-164
    Grammar, *see also*
    Historical perspectives, 79
    Language acquisition, Spanish vs. English, 27, 38
    Pronouns,
        Gustar, 49

　　　　　Subject, 74
　　　　　Question words, 34
　　　　　Reading in Spanish in five minutes, 1-2
　　　　　Tú vs. Usted, 11
　　　　　Using two last names, 5-6
　　　　　Usted vs. Tú, 10-11
　　　　　Verbs, *see also*
　　　　　Vowels, 1
Spanish-speaking
　　　Countries,
　　　　　Facts, 36, 53, 54, 82, 100, 101, 120
　　　　　History of, 35, 79
　　　　　People throughout the Americas, 19
　　　　　　　36, 53, 54, 82, 100, 101, 120
Spelling, phrases, 60
Stores, Grocery scavenger hunt, 131-134
Styles, communication, 118
Subject pronouns, 74
Summary, 176
Survey, welcome to Spanish, Intro

T

Tardiness, 91
Ten ideas to continue learning in the future, 129
Tener = to have, 74-75
The, Four ways of saying, 41
Things you like to do, 49-51
Throughout the Americas, speaking Spanish, 79
Tic-Tac-Toe, game 15, 108
Time,
　　　Phrases 95
　　　Telling 88-89
To be, the verbs, ser vs estar, 104-106
Toma Todo, game directions, 40
Tongue twisters, 60
Tongue muscle, roll R, 2
Tour, book, Intro
Tourist vocabulary,
　　　Directions, 72
　　　Restaurants 114, 119
Translation exercise, 21, 43, 66, 89, 110, 112, 130
Travel,
　　　Agency final project, 165
　　　Advice and etiquette, 123
　　　Holidays, 91, 129
　　　Restaurant, 114, 119
　　　Schedules / Tips, Latin America, 113, 123
　　　Tourists in Puerto Rico, 112
　　　Weather, 94
True/False game, 107
Tú vs. Usted, 11

U, V

Uruguay, 81, 101-102
Useful restaurant lingo, 114, 119
Using two last names, 5-6
Usted vs. Tú, 11
Variations in the Spanish language,
　　　Slang, regional dialects, 38
　　　Cultural communication styles, 118
Venezuela, 81-83
Verbs,
　　　Basic conjugation in present tense, 124-127
　　　-ar present tense, 124-127
　　　-er present tense, 124-127
　　　Estar = to be, 104-106
　　　Gustar = to like, 49-51
　　　Ir = to go, 77
　　　-ir present tense, 124-127
　　　Present tense, 124-127
　　　Querer = to want, 76
　　　Ser vs estar – to be, 104-106
　　　Reflexive verbs, 89
　　　Tener = to have, 74-75
Vowels, 1

W, X, Y, Z

Weather, 94
Welcome to Spanish survey, Intro
Why Spanish is spoken throughout the Americas, 79

GRACIAS

Spanish Chatbook is dedicated to the many people around the world that are working very hard to support their families and learn another language. We hope to build bridges through communication and connect our global society. Now you will be able to speak another language and get to know a new "amigo" or "amiga." Gracias y saludos to our family and friends, son Jaden, daughter Elena, our students and future travelers everywhere. Thanks to Indira Engel, Gonzalo Baron, Vieva McClure, Curtis Grubb and Wendy Biernbaum. An extra thanks to our parents and grandparents who have been amazing role models for us and have taken care of our children while we worked on the book. Thank you for helping us make our dreams become realities. To our readers and Spanish students, thank you for taking your time and putting in the effort to learn Spanish. Feel free to visit our Web site, SpanishChatCompany.com, to give us feedback, or ask questions. If you have any suggestions or changes for a future edition, just let us know. Try out our *Spanish Chatbook 2* for even more conversation and practice with key verbs. We would love to hear testimonials of how this *Spanish Chatbook* has helped you. Keep practicing and keep smiling. Your journey has just begun. Enjoy the adventure! ¡Buen Viaje!

ONLINE GAMES, FLASHCARDS,
ACTIVITIES & VIDEOS

SPANISHCHATCOMPANY.COM

MINI CHATBOOKS